Redneck Dystopia
People's Socialist Republic of the US

David Xu

Copyright © 2020 David Xu

All rights reserved. No part of this book may be reproduced or transmitted in any form or by any means, electronic or mechanical, including photocopying, recording or by any information storage and retrieval system without permission in writing from the publisher.

Mountain View Press—Ashland, PA
ISBN: 978-0-9999035-1-3
Library of Congress Control Number: 2020909864
Title: Redneck Dystopia
Author: David Xu
Digital distribution | 2020
Paperback | 2020

On the cover:
Idi Amin from Uganda, Karl Marx from the Soviet Union, Joseph Stalin from the Soviet Union, and Mao Zedong from China

Other books by David Xu:

Easy Eddie Books One, Two, and Three and Orphans In The Barn

Dedication

This book is dedicated to all hard working Americans. They believe in the ideals that set up this great country in 1776. The United States is about free people, equal people, God the creator, personal responsibility, government by the people, and the pursuit of happiness. The hard workers made America great and free.

The hard workers reject big and wasteful government, lazy government workers, full-time politicians, long-term politicians, high taxes, and social control. That is not what America is about. Hard workers and capitalism must prevail and be celebrated. Most immigrants come here to work hard and live the American dream. God help the American workers!

Contents

Dedication v

Introduction ix

Chapter One 1
The 2020 American Election 1

Chapter Two 29
The 2021 Left Turn and Split

Chapter Three 61
Socialism Light in 2022

Chapter Four 81
Socialism Medium in 2023

Chapter Five 98
Socialism Heavy in 2024

Chapter Six 122
The 2025 American Police State

Introduction

America was founded on the idea that individual freedom is the key. Limited government by the people is the best situation for a society. This basic framework lasted until many bad, myopic, and selfish politicians realized that they can tax, borrow, and spend to divide citizens and buy votes.

All characters in this book are composite. Some are based on Joseph Stalin, Idi Amin, Mao Zedong, Caligula, and a few others combined. This is fiction. Opinion is mixed with fact in some parts.

The colonies and the United States have been the freest and most prosperous society since the settlers came ashore in Jamestown, Virginia in 1607. I would say that America's golden constitution mostly contained government and allowed for massive business success for 243 years from 1776 until 2019. The US is by far the most successful nation ever to grace the face of the Earth. There is a reason for that. It is no accident.

America's founding fathers set up the nation to avoid a left or right dictatorship that would abuse the citizens. They learned how to achieve law and liberty from the great United Kingdom and what to do and not to do. There would be no kings and queens in America.

They believed that the three equal branches would ensure limited or small government. They were wrong and would be shocked at how so many selfish folks get elected over the years and passed laws to gain more and more power, money, and fame by ignoring and subverting the constitution. The penalty for treason is death and should be applied if necessary as per the constitution.

Many current-day politicians are like FDR (known liar) who was elected by pushing his socialist policies in 1933. These selfish politicians use lies and exaggeration to gain power during hard times. They prey on uneducated and poor voters to give socialism or communism a chance. They do not believe in the United States constitution or obey their oath of office to defend it. All US citizens should read history to realize why we are so free. Capitalism and limited government are the keys.

These bad actors hide the fact that capitalism began in Europe only about 300 years ago and has lifted billions of poor people up. Homo sapiens or humans have been around about 400,000 years and their natural state was to be in severe poverty. The ignorant and selfish politicians hide the fact that socialism and communism have always failed and killed over 100 million people so far.

FDR helped some educated leftist groups take over government and universities. FDR and his friends promoted many dumb and wasteful laws like paying farmers not to farm on their land. These socialists ruin the incentive to work hard and that is terrible for any nation.

He also had full-time employees (checkers) check on the farmers to ensure they were not cheating. He also had full-time positions for checkers to check on the checkers who were checking on the farmers.[3] How about that for efficient government at work? From 1933 until today, the big government folks have been expanding the power and control of the politicians and bureaucrats by giving away free stuff to buy votes. This has hurt the hard working Americans and plunged the country heavily into debt. This has disaster written all over it.

This book forecasts what could happen if radical leftist Democrats took over the government and destroyed capitalistic America. It is not about Democrats and Republicans who agree that a free enterprise USA is best as mandated in the US Constitution. It is about a leftist person or group with absolute power over the government and the citizens.

Despite the corrupt leftists, America has helped more people around the globe than any other nation from 1776 until today. The citizens and government of the United States are very generous with those in need. There is no reason to replace capitalism.

I use the word redneck as a compliment. To me, it means someone who works hard and plays hard and probably did not go to college. Going to college does not make you better than anyone. Many hard workers do not attend college and do not mind paying taxes, but do mind supporting a lazy and corrupt governing elite and their children. Look at the protests around the world.

Rednecks reject full-time or part-time politicians buying the votes of lazy folks who want free stuff. Using tax money from workers to help others is fine, but not on a long-term basis. Why are the politicians full-time in DC? Those jobs used to be part-time until the 1950s. Why do we not have term limits?

Most rednecks and college graduates alike want to live the American dream of buying a nice car, owning a great house, and enjoying a loving family. They just want the government folks to protect the homeland, enforce equal rights, keep taxes low, run the government, plan for the long term, and shut up.

They do not want the politician to confiscate their money through high taxes and get on TV all the time and brag about giving it to others. President Obama was great at doing this while implying that most Americans were racist and dumb for rejecting his ridiculous and unconstitutional socialist ideas and policies.

A redneck to me may be a hardworking blue-collar person who did not attend college. Rednecks probably would be unhappy living in the dystopia described in this book. Perhaps they would be frightened by a huge government that despises them.

Rednecks do not know about wine and cheese and rednecks do not care about wine and cheese. Rednecks do not know about ballet and opera and rednecks do not care about ballet and opera. They love God, American success, power, and freedom.

Every redneck I have ever met is patriotic, loves the USA, and has a great sense of humor. Most rednecks believe in God, Jesus, and The Bible. I am a Redneck at heart. They volunteer to help others less fortunate with time and money. Long live the redneck and a free, strong, and capitalistic United States of America!   - Dave

Chapter One
The 2020 Election

"The natural liberty of man is to be free from any superior power on Earth, and not to be under the will or legislative authority of man, but only to have the law of nature for his rule,"

Samuel Adams. (4)

The attractive female news anchor on TV can barely stop smiling to read the news. Her network boss and all employees love big government and NYC. They make a lot of money off the status quo of huge government. She is wearing an expensive blue dress with long, brown hair draped down the front. She is so happy to be on TV that she would read anything the producers hand her.

Many in the media and government are pushing America into socialism and/or communism. None of them has ever lived under a socialist or communist regime. They only know the polished idea of big government and do not read history.

"President Donald Trump has lost re-election to Senator Beth Warner! The Electoral College vote stands at 270 for Warner and only 268 for Trump," the journalist proclaims proudly.

Every hair is in place and the makeup cannot be detected on this fabulous night. She and the coworkers will have a great meal at the steakhouse and then attend an election party later tonight to celebrate the big win. Socialist and communist politicians will be there. Some corporate leaders who somehow got elected by boards of directors will be there too. The big government politicians and big business folks have a good thing going. They call it the gravy train and support each other mostly in the dark so common citizens cannot see. The date is November 3rd, 2020.

This is a big change from election night during 2016 when Donald Trump won. The government news anchor on PBS cried on the air. She knew that President Trump would cut back on her socialist propaganda and lifestyle. President Trump was pro-private enterprise worker and anti-lazy government worker. Most importantly, he was anti-socialist, corrupt, and lazy politician.

Many corrupt governors and others in state and local government changed and stuffed ballots for Warner through mail-in voting. They let everyone vote by mail and then easily changed votes and destroyed millions of ballots for Trump. Social Democrats carried the day to enable socialism in America. They hate Trump, capitalism, and Biblical values. The Christians will suffer now.

The Warner campaign had the greatest variety of T-shirts (90). She had to win with this great socialist cause and effort. One says "Impolite Arrogant Women Make History." She made a lot of money selling these products.

She loves the money from her book and T-shirts to fund her lavish lifestyle flying around the world being famous. But she cannot seem to embrace capitalism by giving "free" government health care for people who will not work funded through heavily taxing the working citizens.

Most of the media folks helped hide Warner's mistakes, scandals, and socialist beliefs. They love making a lot of money and pretending to love President Warner and her policies. Socialism is fine with them as long as they prosper while on TV and the internet. The media people have money that buys their freedom and they do not care at all about the hard working Americans with little money.

Over at the Warner campaign headquarters in Boston Beth Warner made a speech. Bernie Sandman almost fell out of his chair applauding the new improved socialist President.

"We vow to reverse the austerity policies of the last four years and redistribute wealth to the people left behind in our country. Together, we have rejected Donald Trump's help the rich and soak the poor experiments. Those trapped in poverty will be our focus. Thank you for your support," President Elect Warner proclaims.

She knows that government got bigger and bigger during the Trump years. Welfare paid for by the hard workers expanded all along from the dumb politicians who traded welfare for votes from many lazy and myopic citizens. President Trump fought it, but the leftists ensured that big government was primary over the citizens. Too many Americans voted for free stuff over the long-term success of our country and prosperity for their children. Socialism and communism have always failed. But Warner and her supporters want to give it one more try.

Many American politicians live by the motto of Gore Vidal, "Never miss a chance to have sex or be on TV." He was a failed left wing politician and writer. They could care less about the long-term success of the United States.

It is not clear how the Warner administration will pay for all her promises during the campaign. Her campaign manager talks about more state control, taxing, and spending. Many business owners and hard workers are frightened about the outcome of the election.

Warner and her team are talking openly about redistributing somebody's wealth. They danced around the subject before the election. Trump and his team talked about the American workers on his election night four years ago.

The Democrats tried to impeach Trump from 2016 until yesterday, but failed. They won tonight. They could prove that he said some dumb things, but could not prove that he should be thrown out of office. Have you heard all the dumb things previous presidents have said?

The Obama regime and deep state actors spied on the Trump campaign, transition team, and presidency. They broke the law to spy on the non-socialists. This level and scope of criminal activity from the federal government employees was shocking. Biden even bragged about his corruption involving his son in Ukraine on TV. Many Americans lost all trust in their huge government and the fools who run it.

Corruption and coups happen all the time in many different nations. Now it is attempted in the United States. It was only a matter of time because the government got too big and powerful.

"This is a clear mandate to move toward socialism and away from corrupt capitalism. Together with our fine unions, we will take our government back. We will take our national treasure back for those left behind," President Warner said.

She is vague with the language. She wants more tax money by confiscating businesses and savings from conservative voters. It is as though she is raising a window blind to let in a lot more socialism. The country had become a dark place from capitalism in her mind.

"The IRS! They're like the Mafia, they can take anything they want!" Jerry Seinfeld. (4)

The thirty page Constitution could not hold back the leftists, socialists, and communists in the White House, Senate, House, and

Supreme Court. The politicians eroded the checks and balances from the founders over several decades.

"I would rather entrust the government of the United States to the first 400 people listed in the Boston telephone directory than to the faculty of Harvard University," William F. Buckley, Jr. (4)

All the leftist government leaders agree that they must march toward communism. This term means many things to many people. The leaders agree that it means order structured from the top of government and common ownership of the means of production. The government must be supreme from now on.

The model for the Warner administration is China. The developmental stage of US socialism begins now with a socialist market economy. One-party rule will ensure that the fruits of selling goods and services will flow into the politician's hands.

The government leaders dream of slush funds at every corporation. This is the Chinese way since 1949. They think about all the great vacations, meetings, and great meals they will have on official government travel around the world. Their time to shine is here. They are building a socialist paradise and in a hurry.

The leaders can dream and talk about moving to communism, but this corrupt socialism will do just fine for a long time. The plan is well-developed, solid, and firm. The leftists will rule for a while now. They caught many moderate Democrats, Republicans, and capitalists napping.

"The most terrifying words in the English language are; I'm from the government and I'm here to help," President Ronald Reagan. (4)

Dale, Sharon, Billy, Gina, and Uncle John are watching TV together after a day of work and school. Dale is a young medical doctor and working for a big hospital chain. He practices family medicine in Orwigsburg, PA. He treats many poor and disabled folks for free just to help out. They live twenty miles north in the mountains of Ashland.

Dale joined the Army ROTC in college and worked hard. The Army paid for medical school and then he pulled four years on active duty to pay the government back.

Sharon is a team leader in the IT department of the county government. She works in the big government building in downtown Pottsville. The county seat is located there under the clock tower. She and Dale are 40 years old now.

Billy is 13 and enjoys baseball, girls, and making odd noises. Gina is 15 and enjoys reading history, poetry, and playing soccer. Both are wise beyond their years from listening to their good and strong Christian parents.

Uncle John is a true American redneck. He dropped out of community college many years ago and started an auto parts store. He is very successful in the brick and mortar store and online selling mostly Chevrolet Nova parts. John is a great story teller and loves a good joke.

John was married and divorced twice. He is very generous and loving, but always had an eye for other ladies. He reads articles and books and is great with practical and physical hard work. He has tons of common sense and helps others all the time.

John made a ton of money and had five employees for years, but downsized to avoid paying so much in taxes. He is tired of paying taxes to dumb politicians who waste the money.

His only employee now is Bo. He has a dragon tattoo on his neck and wears a Santa hat during the Christmas season. He mows grass during the warm months and does very well.

Bo wears his favorite T-shirt all the time. It has a picture of Ronald Reagan and the caption reads "I smell a commie!"

Sharon's mother and John are siblings from a very close family from North Carolina. The mother, Joan, and her husband were in a bad car wreck and the husband died. An opioid addict slammed into the back of the car on Highway 61 in St Clair in front of Walmart.

Joan lives in a very nice retirement home in Cressona. She loves it there with plenty of friends and activities. Some of the older men try to date her, but she only wants to be friends. She enjoys taking the free bus to the mall over on Route 61.

"Boy, we took it on the chin tonight kids. That sucks. Things are going to be a little different around here," John said.

"What do you mean Uncle John? Most of the teachers love Warner," Gina asks.

"This bunch who won does not care much for the private sector folks. They want government to run everything. How do these unqualified fools keep getting elected such as Obama and Biden? Warner and her friends will grow government bigger than Obama ever dreamed. There will be more and more waste and corruption," John explains.

"My history teacher loves Warner. She said that she will increase the funding for the schools and give everyone new laptops," Gina said.

"You have that right. What she means is that Pocahontas will pump plenty of money into the teachers union for free healthcare and retirement for a bunch of lazy teachers. Most teachers are good, but many are just lazy and do not care if you learn anything," John said.

"That Warner woman was dumb and immoral to lie about being a Native American just to get jobs. Do you think our taxes will go up?" Gina asks.

"There is no doubt. I better start accepting more cash and less credit cards and checks to hide some income from these government jokers. Don't tell anyone that. Is your teacher pretty?" John asks.

"Yes, she has long brown hair and jogs all the time. She is single. She coaches volleyball too," Gina responded.

"Ooh, I like that. I do not jog, but I love it when the ladies do. Perhaps I will take in a volleyball game and share with her the virtues of capitalism," John said.

"Please do not mention my name. She is kind of opinionated and will give me bad grades. She said the Chinese government model would work very well here and all business people are greedy and corrupt," Gina said.

"What the hell is she teaching? My taxes pay her sorry ass. I will bring my pocket Constitution on our first date. I can ask her to point out where our constitution supports socialism or communism," John said.

"I would love to see that. She gets mad if you challenge her during her lectures," Gina said.

"You see capitalism aligns the human instinct to take care of yourself through hard work. And through taxes we can also have a good government. The problem is when government gets too big, wasteful, and corrupt many hard workers lose faith. That is where we are tonight," Uncle John said.

"You should teach our history and government classes Uncle John. Our teachers come straight out of liberal colleges. They never ran or owned businesses. They never even worked at a lemonade stand," Gina said.

"Can you put in a recommendation to the principal? I am just joking. I have plenty of money to invest in other businesses, but do not want to pay any more taxes to the dumb politicians. So in my tiny world, I will not create any more jobs for the uneducated folks.

I would invest and create jobs if taxes were low and regulation light. Millions of business owners think like me," John said.

"I understand that completely. I think the people like my teacher do not understand how capitalism with limited government lets the rich, middle class, and poor thrive together," 'Gina said.

"You are very smart from good genes. Many business owners would not invest during the Obama years. He and his gang criticized, abused, harassed, and taxed heavily people with money. Therefore the people needing jobs suffered," John said.

"You would frighten that young teacher. She is half your age. I remember when you played around and yelled at the real estate tax collector," Sharon said.

"How can you sleep at night?" John yelled when he paid his $8,000 real estate tax bill for his house last year in Ashland. The local government charges this tax every year and wastes the money on unnecessary government employees shuffling paper. Meanwhile, the roads and bridges crumble. People renting apartments do not pay or feel the pain of the real estate tax every year and want bigger government with more free stuff.

The socialists and communists have been so angry for the last four years because Hillary Clinton lost the election during 2016. They wanted to continue to dismantle the United States Constitution and the government it set up in order to move toward socialism and stay in power. They want Christians and Christian values out of government and they want them out now.

"Our Constitution was made only for a moral and religious people. It is wholly inadequate to the government of any other," President John Adams in 1800. (4)

The TV camera pans over to the crowd behind the President. Hillary Clinton is sitting there with a big smile in a big red pant suit outfit.

"She looks like a candy apple," John tells everyone.

"Do you mean that she has a big head or is obese?" Dale asks.

"She definitely has a big head and a large body. She and Bill are loving this socialist love festival. The Clinton foundation is back in business for government contracts baby! Fire up the grill!" John said.

Now is their time to expand government so big that the Democrat Party will never lose power again. They will march toward one-party rule as soon as possible. This is the best form of government in their ill informed minds.

They choose to promote only the good things about socialism and suppress the bad. They will lie, cheat, and steal to shield the ignorant masses from the facts such as over 100 million people have died or been killed by socialists and communists.

"This Warner regime will probably be worse than the Obama-Biden regime. Many of them were very anti-Christian, anti-American, anti-constitution, anti-worker, socialist, lazy, corrupt, and racist. They were actually traitors in the White House," Sharon said.

"I agree because they rejected limited government, which is mandated by our wonderful constitution. Do you remember when they tried to get the Little Sisters of the Poor to pay for contraception? That was sick. And they spied on the Trump folks and tried to throw the election during 2016 for crooked Hillary. Then they tried to remove Trump from office with lies and a corrupt special counsel team," Dale said.

The Democrats swept the White House, the Senate, and the House of Representatives on election night. The 52% of citizens who do not pay any federal income tax have prevailed. They want free stuff and a great lifestyle and Warner promised to deliver it to them. They also were tired of the tweets from Trump.

The mainstream Democrats and mainstream Republicans ensured that the fragile democracy lasted 245 years (from 1776 until 2021). They did not agree on a lot, but agreed that a capitalist democracy is better than a left or right dictatorship.

Most Europeans thought America would last no more than a few years. What will they do without a king and queen? How will uneducated people govern themselves?

The American founders were determined not to have a monarchy dominating a working class and poor. Thomas Jefferson saw this nonsense up close while in France in 1784.

"I was much an enemy of monarchy before I came to Europe. Now I am ten thousand times more so since I have seen what they are," Thomas Jefferson.[1] He saw rich, lazy, dumb, drunken, sexual, and immoral folks having fun in government and doing nothing to improve society.

The Americans rejected both left and right dictatorships several times over the years. Socialists, communists, and every other type ran for President, the House, and the Senate. Very few were elected thank God.

Many Americans have lost interest in history. Recent research found that people in 49 of the 50 states cannot pass the citizenship test given to naturalized citizens.[2] The country pays a big price for this ignorance. Many Americans favor socialism or communism and have no idea what they mean for the common man or woman.

The American democracy is over now. Free enterprise is gone. The state or Party is supreme over the individual now. Socialism is here for a while. All citizens will suffer from this foolishness.

The old style Democrat would reject a group dictatorship that abolishes all welfare. The old style Republican would reject a group dictatorship that actively promotes a boy becoming a girl. The Bible provides rules for behavior and most Americans used to agree to disagree on many topics and keep politicians out of personal behavior or social control. Those days are over with big government fools running the show.

The radical Democrats have high jacked the party and now have power. It took many decades for them to achieve total control of

America. Their day is here and they will enjoy it.

"The public school leaders, principals, parents, and teachers have failed to educate the youth on basic American history. Ignorant folks are trying to tear down our history rather than learn from it," Dale said.

"The government employees and politicians cannot do anything right now and they want to take over health care and many businesses. Yeah right! I recall the shooting at the Navy base in Florida by the Saudi in 2019," John said.

"Yeah, that was terrible. He and his friends were radical and violent Muslims from Saudi Arabia. Our government was training them how to fly airplanes," Sharon said.

"I read that the shooter was able to purchase the 9mm Glock pistol legally because Florida gave him a hunting license. (8) These government fools are something else!" John said.

"The Pentagon leaders and politicians bare some blame because they have rules where most soldiers and sailors cannot carry their pistols on base. They are like sitting ducks even today thanks to the liberal fools in government," Dale said.

Most Democrats and Republicans reject the blaming of immigrants for America's problems. Most immigrants work hard and came here to escape corrupt socialist, communist, or dictatorship-type places.

It is ironic that now many are thinking about leaving the United States of America because the leaders just took a hard left-hand turn. It is government's purpose to organize the community, keep the people safe, and create and enforce policies. There are about 200 nations on Earth balancing individual freedom and state authority.

Many leaks are coming out from the transition team in the District of Columbia. Republicans and moderate Democrats can sense a hard left turn is coming for the country. Many hope for just a little more government and free stuff.

Sharon reads an article about the United Kingdom. It is about how conservatives led the country to join what would become the European Union (EU) in 1973. This reminds her of right now and how many Republicans voted for Warner out of disgust for Trump. Trump was their only hope to keep America capitalistic and they blew it.

The similarity is that many conservatives regretted supporting the great European socialist project back then and up until now. The Brits voted to exit the socialist EU in 2016. Now many conservatives have buyers remorse for voting for Warner and her push for the great American socialist project.

John and his friend Pat are talking at the auto shop about J. Edgar Hoover, big government and women.

"I do not know how the Americans missed it. How can they want big government when you have bad examples like J. Edgar Hoover at the FBI?" John said.

"Hoover, now he was a character. How long was he the leader of the FBI? Oh yeah, 37 long years!" Pat said.

"I read that whenever any agent found pornography when conducting raids that had to give it to him personally. The guy loved porn for his own consumption and to blackmail others," John said.

"What is a damn shame is that he could have had so many beautiful women. Thousands were drawn to this powerful idiot," Pat said.

"Why in hell did the politicians keep him in charge of the FBI for so long and not put him in jail," John said.

"He had porn, money, and sex scandals on all those politicians. What a dystopian nightmare," Pat said.

"He loved dogs, men, and cross dressing. I bet he made parties interesting. But I bet everyone was afraid to tell him anything," John said.

"The dumb politicians were so afraid of him that they let him rule until he died. He died in office during 1972," Pat said.

"There are so many Hoovers hunkered down in government jobs for 30-40 years doing nothing right now. It is a damn shame that normal working folks have to pay tax to support all these fools. It is almost impossible to fire them," John said.

Hoover was devious, unethical, and hated women. He fired all female agents in 1924. He also banned the future hiring of women. (5)

"If you want to know the caliber of our folks in the White House, Senate, and House just ask yourself one question. Why do they keep Hoover's name on the FBI building?" John said.

"I know what you mean. The worst folks get elected such as Obama. His wife is the worst. She said the first time she was proud of America was when her dumb husband got elected. I wonder if she is just ignorant of our great history of helping hundreds of millions have freedom or just racist or just a liar who will do or say anything to get her husband elected," Pat said.

"The sad thing is that many uneducated citizens believe whatever the stupid politicians and their spouses say. I guess many, many Americans will vote for anyone who gives them free stuff. The myopic and foolish masses sure have in a bind now," John said.

"I read that Michelle Obama had a sweet job at a hospital where she did not show up very often just because her husband was in the Senate. The hospital paid her a lot of money. The hospital did away with the position after she left," Pat said.

Sharon, Dale, Gina, Billy, and Joan drive to the King of Prussia Mall for some Christmas shopping. Sharon gives the kids $100 each to buy gifts.

They hang out next to Santa and his wife making money taking pictures with the kids. Gina and Billy are too old for that, but all four love to hear the children ask for odd gifts from Santa.

The mall is packed and the economy is still good. The Trump gang has stimulated animal spirits by reducing business taxes and regulation. Business owners are hiring people like crazy and all is good. Most Americans are not thinking about the socialist storm brewing.

"What do you want from Santa little boy?" Santa asks the chubby boy dressed in camouflage with an orange hat.

"I want a deer head!" the child asks Santa. He is smiling ear to ear.

His dad explains that the kid loves the mounted deer heads at home. He skips asking for a gun and hunting lessons and jumps ahead for the mounted deer.

"What does the little girl want for Christmas?" Santa asks the girl with thick glasses and a bow on her head.

"I would really love a big chef salad Santa," the child informs Santa. She is very serious.

The mother turns red and explains that the child is very hungry. The poor girl wanted to eat before they got into the long line. The mother insisted that they take the cute pictures first.

The Democrat Party leaders call for an economy based on socialism. They are really moving toward market distorting state socialism for now. The national government will own or control most businesses soon.

They preach about socialism to get the votes and never mention corruption. It is funny how the socialists talk of getting to communism, but they never quite make it to where they live like the common man and woman. Most socialist and communist leaders or cheerleaders live like kings and queens.

Millions of Americans lost faith in the church. There were scandals in the Catholic church and others. Pope Francis promoted socialism and criticized capitalism and that hurt his support and appeal.

The Pope and his team got caught in 2019 using Peter's Pence charitable gifts to pay for administrative expenses. Only about 10% of the gifts went to the poor. (8) It seems that the Holy See is a fan of big government and waste just like the other socialist government leaders around the globe. The Vatican folks have been funding great full-time jobs in Rome at the expense of the poor.

The Vatican is running big budget deficits and was suspended from the international network of anti-money laundering watchdogs too. (8) All this and the London real estate scandal and the perverted priests hurt the credibility of the Pope and his operation. Many people turned to the government and socialist politicians for money and support. Many folks forgot the great living principles in The Bible.

Pope Francis was one of the weaker popes, but at least he did not boil any critics in oil in public like one pope did. Pope Leo X was a bad seed in 1520 for selling indulgences (relief from damnation in the afterlife) to buy art. (5)

"Most of the government socialists, media workers, and communists love to criticize the church because they see it as competition for funds and influence. Many government people also do not like the Biblical rules of living. They do not want any boundaries on human behavior in order to get votes and power and money. Most of the folks in Hollywood feel the same way. They have a product to sell and cannot offend anyone with a statement of right and wrong," John said.

"I don't understand it. Jack will spend any amount of money to buy votes, but he balks at investing a thousand dollars in a beautiful painting," Jackie Kennedy. (4)

The Federal Reserve socialists helped the Democrats take the House of Representatives during 2018 by raising interest rates four times. That slowed the economy and hurt the Trump gang, Republicans, and conservatives.

That election enabled the leftist Democrats to waste a lot of tax money on impeachment proceedings.

Many Federal Reserve leaders and employees love big government and all the great jobs and free trips. There is a whole industry of high-paying and unnecessary jobs associated with the Federal Reserve. The Fed has about $2 trillion of US dollars in circulation and this helps create inflation.

The Federal Reserve folks tried to get Hillary Clinton elected in 2016, but she and the husband were just too offensive for the voters. They kept interest rates low so Obama and company could borrow, tax, and spend to buy many votes. That nonsense lasted eight years and the federal government debt doubled to $20 trillion. Everyone knows that high debt is risky for a nation, business, or individual.

The House under Nancy Pelosi fought every conservative action by the Republicans and Trump from 2018 until 2020. She and her team wanted so much to continue down the socialist road as with Obama and Clinton.

"The socialists at the Federal Reserve try to hide their politics, but make mistakes. Janet Yellen got caught hanging out with Obama and the Democrats all the time and ignoring the Republicans. Trump knocked her off her throne of money and power during 2018," John said.

"I remember when that big Democrat Yellen caused a stir when she had armed guards and huge black SUVs get her in the mornings and deposit her in the afternoons in a normal neighborhood near DC. The neighbors complained. Who the hell does she think she is? Why does she need all this security?" Sharon asks.

The door has a small sign on it that reads "Transition." It is on the fourth floor of the Pentagon. Inside many high-level socialist workers for the campaign are planning and coordinating to take over the government. All political appointees at the Pentagon and all cabinet level departments will be replaced with proven socialists or communists the day after the inauguration.

This clean sweep has never happened before. The leftists who won the White House will remove all moderate Democrats, Republicans, and others immediately upon taking power. They learned from Obama and Trump that allowing dissidents within the government leads to the delay and defeat of abrupt policy changes.

CEO pay in the United States is at 376 times the average worker. The number is 68 in Japan. (5) The voters are sick of this and revolted against the crony capitalism by Democrats and Republicans. The politicians, federal laws, and Securities and Exchange Commission allow this in exchange for campaign contributions and support. Many CEOs and politicians are great friends mostly behind the scenes.

The US Constitution and 27 amendments were supposed to secure the blessings of liberty. But many people lost faith in the government and its leaders. There were too many corrupt and/or myopic politicians, business leaders, media leaders, and voters. Many Americans assumed that the free-enterprise democratic republic would last forever. They were wrong.

Chapter Two
The 2021 Left Turn and Split

On inauguration day, January 12th, 2021, President Warner and the Congress pass several laws. They wrote the laws in secret between the election in November and now. The radical Democrats control government now. They knew Obama was a step in the right socialist direction and celebrated him, but he was too weak and slow for them.

The myopic politicians always divide groups to get votes. Obama blamed the black citizen's problems on the white citizen. Warner blamed the millennial's problems on the older baby boomer. She rode the OK Boomer sentiment all the way to the White House.

Part of the problem is that millions of older Americans did not work hard enough or save enough for retirement. Now the politicians are more than happy to provide subsidized or free Medicare, Medicaid, and Social Security for this group paid for by the younger workers.

The older folks get free stuff and the politicians get votes in order to keep their power and money. Social Security was never meant to be a retirement program. It was meant to be a supplemental retirement program. Tens of millions of Americans failed to be self sufficient and now want tax money from the hard workers. The politicians are forcing the workers to resent the receivers of their tax money. This was never a problem with limited government and low taxes.

John and Gina head down Route 61 to have pancakes and sausage at the local diner. The breakfast is always great there. He is taking her to school for an event in his turbo diesel Ford truck. He loves the truck because it is very powerful and drives it like a sports car.

On day one of the new administration, emergency orders were sent out to transfer money and control from privately owned projects to socialist government projects. The government confiscated many distribution warehouses across the nation for NSA operations.

The Party can scan laptops, smartphones, and other devices from these warehouses. The authorities begin to insert chips into criminals in order to follow and listen to them. This technology helps the government reduce the number of free capitalist rebels.

"How strangely will the tools of a tyrant pervert the plain meaning of words!" Samuel Adams. (4)

Government doctors put the criminals asleep upon arrest and insert the chips. The prisoner is told that they removed a cyst or tumor free of charge. Most of the victims do not know about the microchips inside them. This is covered under Medicare For All.

"What is that Uncle John? That building is huge! There used to be a mall there before Obama and his war on coal," Gina asks.

They are driving from Ashland through Frackville on the way to Pottsville to the high school. A huge warehouse was built behind the McDonald's last year beside Highway 81.

"Well the sign implies that it is a food distribution center for grocery stores. But you will not see much food coming or going. It is really part of the National Security Agency. They are building these warehouses all across the nation to spy on everybody," John explains.

"That is sick. What is wrong with the politicians? Are they ignorant about America's success and freedom?" Gina said.

"Many are ignorant, but many just hide the good history of capitalist America. They only love the power, fame, and money in politics. Watch what you say on the phone and online," John said.

"They are like evil contestants for prom king or head cheerleader at a dystopian high school. Those kids will cut off your arm if you get in their way," Gina said.

"Many free enterprise enthusiasts are going to jail now. The government folks keep it quiet for now. The police plant fake evidence and falsely imprison good people. They took a few friends already," John said.

"I guess the media help to keep it quiet. Most journalists have been sympathetic to socialism for decades," Gina said.

"Boy, you know a lot for a youngster. You are strong and Christian and will be fine. Did you feel the turbo kick in? I am going to empty that syrup bottle on those beautiful pancakes," John said.

"I bet those commies will take your truck pretty soon. The climate change radicals are in charge now. You will be on the bus Uncle John," Gina said.

"The radical Democrats won by signing up illegal immigrants and convicted felons to vote. By the time the lawsuits catch up,

President Warner will have packed the Supreme Court with radical leftists. The high court will approve anything by that time," John said.

"That is so wrong. The Supreme Court justices should only approve laws if they are within the bounds of the constitution. That is how we continue as a great, free, and capitalistic society," Gina said.

"Yes, you are right. President Trump appointed some justices who respect the constitution, but Clinton and Obama found some scoundrels who love socialism and communism just a little too much. They do not give a damn about our constitution. There are many traitors within our government," John explains.

Most Americans lost confidence in their government. The Democrats and Republicans in DC and in many statehouses enriched themselves with full-time positions and did not care about normal, hardworking citizens. Government is so big now that it is more important than individual freedom and rights. The majority of voters want to try a new form of government and throw away the constitution. This is going to be a bumpy ride.

Thousands of judges are detained the day after the inauguration. The charges vary and are totally fabricated. All of the criminals are conservative or Republican. The charges stick and the sentences are long. The transition team performed very well regarding the judiciary.

Law number one declares a national emergency and part one is top-secret. Only the gang of eight (the top leaders of the House and Senate in the Democrat Party) know what is in the law. The law has two parts: part one is top-secret and part two is unclassified. No Republicans can read the top-secret part of the law and none voted for any of it.

What we do know is that it deals with national security. Part one declares climate change an emergency. The politicians in the House and Senate are working out what is to be banned and what is allowed. Cars, trucks, boats, planes, cows, coal, oil, natural gas, motorcycles, etc are all on the table.

AOZ lost her re-election in New York. She says dumb stuff all the time. She lost many voters by declaring that the world will be over in 12 years if we keep our cars and cows. President Warner makes her the EPA Administrator. Earth Day to most Americans means things like cutting back on trash bags, but to Warner and AOZ it means socialists controlling all three branches of government and most businesses.

The Republicans get on TV and the internet and howl with disapproval. It does no good, the election is over and the Democrats have been sworn in. They can do anything they want.

Law number two increases the members of the Supreme Court from nine to twenty-five. FDR tried this communist trick back in the 1930s, but most politicians and citizens rejected it. Trump moved the court to the right with three judges who abide by the constitution and the leftists pitched a fit.

Increasing the judges on the Supreme Court is the easiest route to total domination for the Democrats. Doing so only requires a simple majority in the House and Senate and the President's signature. A Constitutional Amendment requires a 66% vote in the House and Senate and must be ratified by 75% of the states. This is almost impossible in today's partisan environment.

The Supreme Court has at different times had six, seven, and nine members. They have approved many unconstitutional laws over time that expanded government, including many from FDR. Obamacare is another example which cost taxpayers billions of dollars for free health care going to many lazy people with cable TV and nice cars. Hard working Americans view this as grossly unfair.

"To live under the American Constitution is the greatest political privilege that was ever accorded to the human race," President Calvin Coolidge. (4)

You can only expand the government so much if you go by the constitution. It mandates three equal branches, free enterprise, states rights, and limited government. The liberals have been cheating on this for decades with judges who approve of unconstitutional laws to expand government power and control.

"Three groups spend other people's money: children, thieves, and politicians. All three need adult supervision," Dick Armey.[4] Perhaps the leftists never realized this nugget.

The Supreme Court suddenly has 6 conservatives and 19 radical leftists. It only took one month for the President to nominate them and for the Senate to confirm them.

They can approve any government-expanding law that the Democrats pass. They have lifetime tenure (a defect in the

Constitution from 1789). Folks died young back then.

Several top Republicans quietly sell any investments within the reach of the US government. They know that things are moving fast in the wrong direction. They put their domestic houses up for sale.

All of the socialist utopia movement was working fine until Trump won the White House in 2016. He and his team fought and reversed some of the worst leftist laws and rules of the Obama regime. The country was marching slowly and secretly toward socialism when Trump and some other conservatives were elected during 2016.

That is why the leftists are so mad now. They knew that Clinton would have completely transformed the United States from capitalism to socialism/communism during her four or eight years in charge. They were devastated when their corrupt candidate lost the election.

The leftists have been trying to turn America into a socialist paradise since at least 1933 and the election of the rich, serial liar FDR. Most citizens were afraid of communism by learning about the evil Stalin and Mao gangs during the 1950s and 1960s. The capitalist system of the USA remained intact until the LBJ regime came to power after Oswald shot JFK.

With the War on Poverty came more spending, borrowing, and more power for the government fools. Most unions have always been corrupt and then they helped elect more and more leftists in order to get free health care and retirement for government workers. Many union workers are good and work hard.

Most unions are unnecessary now because there are plenty of laws to protect the workers. Even the leftist FDR opposed unions representing government workers. This is a conflict of interest where union members vote for Democrats and Democrats give them more pay and benefits.

The US government and politicians spent and borrowed so much that finally in 1971 the Nixon gang abolished the gold standard.(5) Up until this time, you could exchange every US dollar for a piece of gold. Now there is no gold standard and nothing backs up the US dollar.

The big government folks in Congress created the Federal Reserve in 1913. This group supports a domineering government by printing money. They also loan money to the other parts of the government by buying US Treasury bonds.

It is one part of government loaning money to the other part in order to spend and buy votes. This causes inflation and has ruined many corrupt governments and nations around the world.

The Fed geniuses printed about $12 trillion from 2008 until 2018. By comparison, all the gold ever dug up out of the ground globally adds up to $7 trillion. This was always risky and dumb if you take the long view as an adult always should.

The Federal Reserve leaders, families, and friends fly out to Jackson Hole, WY and have a great time every year spending government money. They pontificate on how smart they are and how great their monetary policy is. This wasteful government department is not authorized in the Constitution. Fed policies have helped somewhat with depressions and recessions, but they have done a lot of damage also. Many employees in the Fed love big and wasteful government paid for by the workers.

President Jackson shut down the predecessor of the Federal Reserve in 1833. He and his supporters believed that the bank would harm personal and economic freedoms.

Top-secret meetings and sessions of Congress are going on. The Socialist Democrats pass a law to repeal the Second Amendment to the Constitution. The right to bear arms lasted from 1791 until now (230 years). It only took two months to get a majority of the House and Senate and for 75% of the states to ratify it.

A voluntary buyback is announced by the government. Millions and millions of Americans collect $500 for each pistol and rifle they turn in to the government. The money is tax free for the individual.

The constitution says nothing about taxing Peter to pay Paul. From 1960 until 2020, the politicians have been taxing, spending, and borrowing to buy votes like crazy. It was not too bad when they ran small deficits each year, but by 2020 the deficits were $1 trillion each year.

"A government that robs Peter to pay Paul can always depend on the support of Paul," George B. Shaw.(4)

This spending on transfer payments, free stuff, and welfare has pitted brother against brother and family against family for no reason. The only reason this happened is because politicians spent like drunken sailors to get into power and stay there.

Now the Democrats employ a great way to increase their funds. Up until now they tax and spend and borrow to buy votes. They get plenty from corporate lobbyists.

The Democrat Party won many votes by focusing on personal identity, being victims of racism, having a global worldview, and enjoying free stuff. Most of the Democrats running to be the nominee of their party in 2019 talked about jacking up taxes on the rich to transfer major cash to the middle class and poor.

Gross Domestic Product (GDP) is the sum of goods and services produced per year. Last year the US GDP was $21 trillion and the highest of the 200 nations on Earth.(5) The federal government took in $4 trillion in taxes and spent $5 trillion on many dumb programs.

Part of their national security law includes a provision to tap into and control and eventually own more businesses. This is the Chinese model. The politicians will infect the boards of huge US companies and pay the federal government dividends from the capitalists.

This scheme will bring in much more money than the mere $4 trillion they brought in last year. The corruption will go through the roof. This is the Chinese Communist

Party model on steroids because America is much more successful and rich than China.

Party officials will sit on the board of directors of all US companies with more than 50 employees. The Party officials are in many departments of the companies to suck up money to support the lazy and corrupt politicians in DC and their families and friends.

The candidates running for the Democrat Party nomination talked or alluded to some of this during 2020 while they were trying to beat Trump. The hard working citizens and Republicans just did not take the threat to free enterprise seriously and thought Trump would win.

Now the country is divided. There are 70 million conservative voters and their families. There are 72 million liberal voters and their families. There are 320 million Americans in the 50 states.

There are 30 million illegal immigrants in the country thanks to an open Mexican border for decades. The Trump gang closed some holes in the fence and laws, but they just kept coming in. Most of these people do not speak English and cost the workers of America $60 billion per year in welfare like housing and food and education. This has been going on for decades and helped the Democrats win elections and power. All illegal immigrants are granted full citizenship this year by the top-secret law. They owe everything to the Democrat Party. They came from terrible and corrupt countries for a better life.

Most wanted and thought they could work hard and succeed in a capitalist dream country. Most are Catholic and do not like it when socialists and communists crack down on religion.

Law number three outlaws the Republican Party, creates a thirty-hour work week, creates a universal basic income, and raises taxes effective immediately. The law does other things that move the country hard to socialism and communism overnight. The Supreme Court will approve anything Congress passes. This is the highest court in the land.

The Party will not talk about it but, it has only been 300 years since billions of people around the world worked hard and created a middle and upper class. This is due to the capitalist governing model.

Before that time, kings and queens ruled many different kingdoms and had all the power and riches. There was no middle class and only the rich and the desperately poor.

The kingdoms and the church used to imprison and execute people for all kinds of things. As societies developed into capitalist situations they created the rule of law and stopped killing people for so many reasons.

There used to eight deadly sins going back at least 2,000 years. They were pride, greed, lust, envy, gluttony, wrath, sloth, and sadness. The offenses were vague and used to destroy people if the rich people did not approve of them. The poor suffered so much until capitalism helped people work hard and rise up.

Can you imagine that? The church and government used to put folks in prison or kill them for being sad and negative all the time. Pope Gregory I took sadness/sorrow, despair/melancholy off the list in AD 590.

Now the Democrat Party and its leaders ignore the great history of free enterprise and move to a system where government owns and controls the means of production. It is a version of the old king and queen model where a small group controls the larger group. The group communist dictatorship worked well for China for about 70 years and then the people got sick of it. The government leaders always say they are equal to the poor, but live like kings and queens behind big walls.

Conflict will occur peacefully in a democracy through the political process with free enterprise or in the streets with socialism and communism. The history has always worked out this way. The Democrat Party members love communism today because they do not read and are ignorant of history. Or perhaps they just really believe in the ideology and think that is has never been implemented correctly.

The President, House, and Senate declare that anyone with net worth over $1 million must donate the excess wealth to the federal government. This money is given to the poor and lazy citizens and not for any work. This will fund big raises for union government workers and politicians. The government goes on a hiring binge during January 2021.

Many business folks and their families panic. They try to transfer their stocks, bonds, and cash out of the country. But the Democrats have them trapped. They hired hundreds of thousands of government IRS agents who prevent most transfers.

The rich people try to sell their houses, but there are not enough buyers. House prices throughout the country take a nosedive in the buyers market. They cannot ship their house to a capitalist country. It is too late to keep their wealth.

The people with money stop investing in businesses. Foreigners stop investing in the United States. Both groups lose confidence that they can make a good profit by investing in this socialist paradise.

Many rich people voted for Warner because they love big government and thought she and her leftists would just raise taxes a bit. They did not dream that the Democrats would confiscate their wealth and destroy the free enterprise system so quickly and efficiently.

The Democrats learned from the Trump gang to move fast when reversing rules and laws. If they move too slow, the next election may throw them out of power. The myopic politicians are the main reason for the decline of the country.

The roads are crumbling with bigger and bigger potholes. The bridges are rusting and becoming dangerous. The Party is spending most tax money on benefits that require no effort or work. This cannot last.

"The American Republic will endure until the day Congress discovers that it can bribe the public with the public's money," Alexis de Tocqueville (4) The Frenchman roamed around America during the early 1800's and wrote "Democracy in America" in 1835. He describes how hardworking Americans willing to move to where the jobs are and liberty were the keys to this successful society. He rejected centralized government because it "excels in preventing, not doing."

The french politicians would have avoided a lot of misery if they had listened to Tocqueville. The bankrupt socialist nation is in deep trouble today. They say that the politician plans for the next election and the statesman plans for the next generation. The statesmen left government a long time ago.

All the spending and borrowing is possible because the United States won WWII in 1945 and Europe and Asia were in ruins. Most nations held the US dollar in their reserves as the most stable currency in the world and invested in America.

America grew very strong with limited government and hard workers and very motivated business folks. Government got out of the way from 1776 until 1933 and the FDR socialist frenzy.

It also helped that many nations have civil wars and coups all the time and are therefore very unstable. Most business owners with money will not invest in unstable countries.

The dictators come in and take over foreign businesses if they do not get paid enough through corruption. Business owners can lose billions of dollars of investment overnight if the dictator turns on them.

Many hard workers and their families move to the southern United States to save some tax money. Most states in the south generate more GDP, have lower taxes, and have more limited government to fund programs than the northern states. The real estate is cheaper too with bigger houses and larger lots.

Tens of thousands of big and nice houses are vacant. The hard workers left in a panic for the south. The Party buses in millions of former illegal immigrants to live in the houses.

The Ministry of Interior puts twenty brand new citizens into each house and provides free power and food and spending money. Luxury neighborhoods begin to deteriorate. The siding gets filthy, the grass grows tall, the roads are cracking, and trash is everywhere.

There are not enough jobs because the folks with money have gone away. The government funds are tight. Socialism takes root quickly if pushed from the top. Many want to work hard, but there are no jobs around.

Many communities start to resemble the dirty and poor areas all over Mexico. The new citizens are quite surprised and disappointed. Most of them speak Spanish and not English. They were told that America is the land of milk and honey with many, many rich people.

A large subdivision near Tamaqua named Eagle Rock has 1,000 luxury homes in it. Rich people from New York City used to keep these places as vacation homes next to a ski resort. The government lets 20 illegal immigrants live in each house now for free.

This is great for the poor immigrants, but The Party will take it on the chin in terms of revenue. The rich folks used to pay $6,000 per year for real estate tax. This was redistributed to poor people in the form of welfare and food stamps.

The Democrat Party no longer takes in the $6 million per year from just this one neighborhood to pay for government programs and welfare. This government confiscation takes place all over the country.

The government even placed twenty illegal immigrants into the former guard shack at the front of the development. The ski resort shut down a while back due to lack of demand laying off many workers.

Many illegal immigrants feel like they are in one of those transporters in Star Trek show. This place resembles Mexico more every day with corrupt politicians, criminals running wild, and no jobs.

Back in Mexico the politicians could not protect them from the drug cartel criminals and now the same holds true for US North. But at least the Mexican government did not bombard them with weird propaganda such as changing your gender is like changing your underwear.

It is kind of like the end of the first Planet of the Apes movies where Charlton Heston and his sexy girlfriend are taking a horse ride on the beach. They discover the Statute of Liberty sunk on the beach. He yells and cries because he realizes that he is back on Earth and the place went down hill after the chimpanzees, orangutans, and gorillas took over from the humans.

I thought he was crying about his sunburn when I was a kid watching the movie in 1968. I know what that is like. He and the woman are wearing skimpy Tarzan outfits in the bright sun for days.

A movement develops in the south. At this time 160 million people live in the south and

160 million live in the north. California is definitely part of the north.

The southern citizens love the idea of limited government that the founders believed in during 1776. The northern citizens love big government where it owns the mean of production and everyone makes about the same amount of money.

Mass protests and secret meetings lead to demands that the southern states secede from the union. It has been 160 years since the south seceded in 1861. The south has an army of one million. The north inherits an army of one million, but has devastated it with huge budget cuts to feed the masses with free food, housing, cellphones, and universal basic income.

Rather than fight another bloody civil war the country splits. The dividing line runs from the southern border of Virginia to California. The capitalists are in the south and the leftists are in the north. Alaska joins Canada and Hawaii stays with the north. Puerto Rico breaks away to form a socialist paradise.

A border wall is built between the north and south. It is thirty feet high and keeps many northern citizens from migrating to the south.

The Democrats used the East German model from 1949.

The Berlin Wall stood between 1961 and 1989 and cut off the communist east from the capitalist west. The communists had to build a barrier to hold its people hostage.

"The Capitalists will sell me the rope we will use to hang them," Vladimir Lenin. He lied and impersonated a democrat to gain power in 1917 and then proceeded to create a communist paradise and kill millions of Russians.

When the United States of America split into two nations it owed $14 trillion to bondholders outside the government. These nations, businesses, and individuals in the US and abroad loaned money to fund government programs. They earned a small amount of interest and the bonds were considered risk-free by the so-called experts because the US had never defaulted on its debt.

Each country owes $7 trillion after the split and each country has its own currency and Federal Reserve Bank.

US North continues to tax, spend, and borrow to fund the socialist paradise. Most workers only pull thirty hours per week and have plenty of money for fun. Many people spend their money on drugs, alcohol, gambling, pornography, and prostitutes.

"America North is a shell of its former self. This is what happens when you have total freedom for 250 years. America South is doing fine," the German Chancellor said last week.

The Germans turned to socialism back in the 1960s. They are no capitalists, but see that the Americans are making the same mistakes that they made.

The German politicians and business folks caused a lot of pain when they promoted diesel vehicles as being good for the environment. They lied on the emissions tests for decades and were caught in 2015. This is what happens when business gets in bed with government.

Many Germans called the Americans dumb for rejecting diesel vehicles. The government put many business people in jail for this scandal, but no government people went to jail.

The North is forced to spend billions and billions paying down the debt of many cities and states. The local politicians have borrowed and spent too much on union employees and massive government operations.

All the bonds from local governments are rated as junk bonds by the international bond rating firms. There are gas pipeline explosions every week around the country because the mayors and city councils did not maintain the pipelines.

The explosion in San Francisco destroyed forty buildings and killed 4,000 people last week. The mayor is calling for the death penalty for the gas company CEO. The mayor hides the fact that she approves the budget for gas line maintenance and cut the subsidies many times. The city selects five of the ten on the utility board of directors.

The local government leaders and bureaucrats mostly control what the public utility companies do. They cut and cut the maintenance budgets to fund free stuff in exchange for votes.

The mayor gave the all clear two days after the gas explosion last week. She did this despite the fact that an expert in the gas company warned that gas levels were too high. Five hundred people died after moving back in.

Crony capitalism is alive and well in the federal, state, and local governments. The politicians have slowly over decades increased the size of government and control over businesses. The corruption, bribes, payoffs, and risk of operations grew steadily.

Millions of citizens get the universal basic income of $1,000 per month from the government. Many uneducated, lazy, and mentally ill live in tent cities. There are huge ones all over the nation. They party every night and have no purpose. Hedonism wins the day with this crowd. Drug use and crime are rampant.

"Where you have the most armed citizens in America, you have the lowest violent crime rate. Where you have the worst gun control, you have the highest crime rate," Ted Nugent. (4)

The politicians have purged Christianity and all religions from the public square. Religion and the rules of the Bible cannot be spoken in public or in the schools and colleges. Most children and adults do not learn the boundaries from the Bible or any other religion.

The Party's position is that anything goes and everything is okay. Any citizen can change their gender and commit crimes at will. The government provides everyone with free health care. This includes elected surgery like wrinkle reduction or sex reassignment surgery as well as surgery for illness and disease.

Millions of criminals are let out of prison because the Democrats declared social justice. The Party position is that most black criminals are in prison due to racist judges, lawyers, and accusers. The Party position is that criminal behavior is not the problem.

Violent and non-violent crime rates skyrocket. The police do not enforce laws against theft below $1,000, urinating in public, and many other crimes.

Party officials and those with money retreat behind tall walled neighborhoods. This is what always happens when neighborhoods or nations go down hill. Look at Somalia. The government secretly passes a law to tax most 401K accounts and IRAs. The tax is 10% of the total if the amount saved is over $200,000. This will hurt the hard working savers and give billions to the politicians to redistribute.

The new tax goes into effect immediately and payable next April when citizens file their taxes. The IRS employees are very happy about this new revenue stream. Government spending is increasing every year on things like subsidies for home heating fuel, bus fare, grocery store food, debt forgiveness, and many other programs. All union government employees will get big raises from this new tax.

Inflation is rising because of many mistakes from the government. The currency is falling in value due to political uncertainty, rising power costs, and a general loss of faith in the country.

Unemployment is rising every quarter. All the government borrowing crowds out business borrowing and investments and job creation are postponed or canceled. Americans who saved money discover many ways to transfer the money out of the country to avoid higher taxes.

International investors are looking elsewhere to growth and profit opportunities. Government wastes money and businesses generate revenue that exceeds expenses and create profit. The investors want low risk and a high return on their money. Government and socialism give you the opposite.

Over in Mountain View, California the government takeover of Google is almost complete. The Party nationalized many businesses with the secret laws passed shortly after the inauguration.

Most of the former Google executives and employees fled to Panama after training their government replacements. They run the government down there and the tax rates are much lower. Panama is now a socialist paradise thanks to Google.

The Party learned how to manipulate search findings from the engineers. The Google engineers learned all the tricks by watching the Chinese Communist Party suppress the citizens for decades. John and Pat are talking about the close relationship between business and government. Many of the founders warned about this collusion against the common man.

"The Trump gang tried to force the Google and Twitter folks to not discriminate against conservatives and Republicans, but failed after four years. The lobbyists, socialists, lawyers, and judges pulled together as a team and won that battle in DC against the common man. All is well now that the hardware and software developed by Google is firmly in government hands," John said.

"The Google liberals and leftists had it made for eight years under the Obama regime. The CEO and his minions had the run of the White House for many years. The campaign donations to the Democrats were very generous. The politicians would not move on anti-trust matters and/or other threats to their business model," Pat said.

"What was President Obama's personal net worth before getting elected to the Senate? What was President Obama's net worth after leaving the White House? Preaching about big government and socialism pays very well indeed for some folks. Why are there no term limits for the House and Senate?" John said.

Twitter is run by the Ministry of Information as is the former Google and all the other social media web sites. Dissent is quickly removed and offenders put in jail or destroyed.

President Warner and her team continue to pump billions into state and local government employee pension funds. She promised to give boatloads of tax money to the government union folks in exchange for votes last year and now the bill is due.

The Democrats have increased pensions for decades without raising taxes to pay for them in most of the fifty states. The reckless politicians also raised the pay for government workers to get elected and to get re-elected. They did not give a damn about the long-term future of the country.

The working class did not pay attention to the overspending by the dumb politicians. Many workers were seduced by free government programs and did not think about the boat loads of full-time government employees they would have to support for decades to run the unnecessary programs.

The Ministry of Information sent in armed agents in the middle of the night to shut down News Corp in Manhattan. Rupert Murdoch abandons the huge headquarters building in New York City and sets up shop in Orlando. Fox News and the Wall Street Journal thrive as usual in US South reporting the truth.

The Democratic Socialist Party leaders force Murdoch to sell the prime real estate in New York to the government for 10% of market value. There can be no non-socialist media firms in the new country. Party officials, government workers and illegal immigrants move into the former News Corp building.

One America News Network abandons its headquarters in San Diego and moves to Miami. The Party raided and confiscated this media outlet's property too. The employees in California, Washington, DC, and New York City sell their condominiums and houses and head to Florida. They lose a lot money on their homes, but the US South is still based on capitalism, freedom of the press, and individual freedom.

Chapter Three
Socialism Light in 2022

The international bond markets stop buying US North bonds. Global investors are spooked with the huge deficits and debt of the country. This triggers immediate spending cuts by The Democratic Socialist Party (The Party). The Democrat party has a new name.

The same thing happened in Greece in 2007, Puerto Rico in 2014, and Venezuela in 2016. The socialists and communists in the United States ignored all of these warnings in order to buy votes and stay in power.

The government continues to confiscate all guns. Soldiers, police, and all government personnel sniff out and take guns from millions of citizens this year. The population must be disarmed under one-party rule anywhere.

Millions of citizens hide their guns and ammunition for a rainy day. There is no way for the socialists to find all the guns. Moderate Democrats are uneasy about the government disarming everyone.

Tens of millions of Americans either looked the other way in order to get free stuff or just did not read and remained ignorant voters. Many are myopic and do not plan for the future. This phenomenon has occurred in many nations in history.

The total debt of the nation stands at $14 trillion now. It is twice the amount of when US North split with US South last year.

Massive riots break out when the Democrats cut the universal basic income from $1,000 per month to $700. The poor, violent, or lazy folks burned many buildings and cars in LA, DC, Houston, and other cities. They like the free money and freedom to do nothing.

The government is listening in on billions of phone calls everyday. The same enthusiastic politicians in charge of this eavesdropping today are the same folks who screamed when the Bush gang gathered only metadata to catch terrorists after 9/11/2001. Millions of citizens are rounded up and sent to prison for talking favorably about capitalism and other vague crimes. Communists and socialists must lie and repress the truth to maintain power. Obama, Biden, and their team were actually traitors in the White House. They worked hard to turn America into a socialist state thereby betraying the US constitution, which mandates limited government by the people. They took an oath to obey the constitution and forgot about it the next day.

"Unfortunately, you've grown up hearing voices that incessantly warn of government as nothing more than some separate, sinister entity that's at the root of all our problems. You should reject these voices," President Obama in 2013.

Obama loves to talk, but would never talk about the NSA complex outside of Salt Lake City, Utah. Behind the concrete walls, tall fences, and roaming gun-mounted armored personnel carriers many government employees (all Party members) run supercomputers that sift through emails and texts looking for anti-socialist comments and plans.

The Party has been planning for civil disobedience for years. Re-education camps have been built outside of Dallas and Atlanta. Each one can house 200,000 criminals.

They are given free cable, food, health care, and exercise equipment. Mandatory classes about peacefully living with your neighbors are given all day long. The prisons fill up within a month.

The government health care workers harvest organs from the prisoners who die in custody. This brings in millions of dollars from selling the organs in other countries. The program is top-secret and run out of the Pentagon.

The bodies are burned after all valuable organs are removed and put on ice for transport on Air Force planes. The family is notified of the death and gets a lovely urn with ashes and that is all. The government offers free urns with your choice of five colors and floral designs.

Many prisoners lose faith in The Party and the socialist government. Most turn Islam to fill the void. This is against the law, but the guards cannot enforce it.

Small-time prisoner clerics indoctrinate their fellow prisoners. Sharia law is taught to be the best governmental system. It is taught that lying is okay if it furthers the religion. Some read the Koran to promote this.

The slaughter of infidels is promoted. Violent folks interpret this in the Koran. Women must be the property of the man.

The newly-minted Muslims create secret mosques in the ghettos when they get out of the re-education camps. The tent cities around the country all have Muslim areas or no-go areas for the security forces.

Last year a few radical Muslims blew up the mayor's office in Savannah to protest inequality and discrimination. They killed thirty government workers in the blast. They are so foolish to think they can overthrow the government.

By this time the government is huge with security cameras on every light pole and spies in every town. There is no way to overthrow The Party.

"Communism is a religion that is inspired, directed, and motivated by the Devil himself who has declared war against Almighty God," Billy Graham. (4)

A few years ago soldiers and other security personnel confiscated all pistols and rifles outside of government control. They went door to door and tent to tent all across the nation. The only people with weapons are in The Democrat Party.

The poor, dumb, and lazy can make pipe bombs and kill a few, but cannot make guns or tanks to take over the government. That train left a long time ago.

"Did you hear about Jim Houser?" Dale asks Sharon at lunch at the diner in St Clair.

"No, what happened?" Sharon asks.

"You know he borrowed a lot of money to open his family practice clinic. The government shut him down yesterday and were trying to force him into a government job. They found him hanging from his belt in the clinic this morning," Dale explains.

"That is terrible! He has a wife and kids. What is going on? This government is out of control!" Sharon said.

"I know. Jim was always so nice and loved his patients. The government folks were forcing him to shut down and would not pay his debts," Dale said.

"Poor thing. He worried about his debt payments. All he wanted was to have a small doctor's office just like his late father had," Sharon said.

"I do not understand The Party. We already have a shortage of doctors int this country. Now they just killed one. The elderly loved Jim," Dale said.

"I read in the newspaper that the government may take over your hospital," Sharon said.

"I know. That would be a disaster. Can you imagine government bureaucrats running a hospital system? I read horror stories about the British national healthcare system all the time," Dale said.

"Yes, the Canadians and the Brits have to wait for appointments sometimes forever. Some people have died waiting for medical care. Why can't government just stay out of things? This nation was founded with limited government," Sharon said.

"I wish we could get out and escape to the south. But if we go, the government will take our house and everything," Dale said.

"I cannot leave my mother either. The government rules prevent her from leaving the retirement home," Sharon said.

"The border is pretty secure too. How would we get by the guards and that huge wall?" Dale said.

The couple holds hands and prays to God and Jesus that something changes. They pray for their family and friends and the American way of life. Capitalism is all they have known and it has been good.

They read many books and articles that lay out why capitalism is the best system because when government gets big people go to jail and people are executed. This has always happened in places like China, Russia, North Korea, Cambodia, and Laos.

Billy walks to Uncle John's auto parts store after school to work his part-time job. While he is walking through downtown Frackville a gang of drug addicts and dealers accost him.

The criminals punch him a couple times and steal his backpack and money. A barber sees the attack and comes to the rescue. He calls the police. The police refuse to do anything since the theft is under $1,000. That is the federal law.

"Are you okay? Let me see your injuries," John said.

"Yeah, they just hit me a couple times. Their eyes were so bloodshot. They looked like zombies in that movie," Billy said.

"You know there was a time when the police would punish punks like that. This is bullshit," John said.

"I wish the police would protect us. I do not trust them anymore," Billy said.

"This is what you get with socialism or communism or whatever the idiots want to call it this week. I am sorry for not being there with you with my little friend," John said.

He shows Billy his small pistol he hides in a hidden pocket in his jacket. John would not hesitate to blow away a criminal who threatens his family.

The ridiculous government employees put people in jail for shooting criminals now days.

But John would gladly do the mandatory six month sentence for this.

"Hey Uncle John, why did you tell me that the Democrat Party keeps raising your taxes?" Billy asks.

"It is all about control. Those government fools want to control everything. Do you remember when you helped me paint my rental house last year?" John asks.

"Yes, that was fun and you gave me a lot of money," Billy said.

"Well, did you see the politicians helping us? Did you see any government or union folks helping us?" John.

"I certainly did not," Billy said.

"I know you did not. But you know what I did see? I saw the dumb politicians on TV that night bragging about spending my tax money on lazy people and drug addicts," John said.

"The government folks abuse and punish hard workers and reward the lazy. That is the way it has always been," John continues.

"You taught me that big government is very wasteful and corrupt. It will always be that way because it is one group spending another group's money," Billy said.

"Yes, government operations are always more wasteful than business operations because it is someone spending someone else's money. You will always be more careful with your own money than spending the money of someone else," John said.

"The government workers should have repaired that pothole a couple years ago. That bad road put you in the hospital after your motorcycle crash," Billy said.

"I remember that well. The roads and bridges are crumbling while the socialists burn our tax money for dumb stuff like free apartments for young idiots. These people sit around and get high and laugh at hard working people going to work," John said.

"She cannot find a sustainable argument that people should be paid for not doing any work," Denis Thatcher said of his wife Margaret Thatcher. She was a very successful, conservative Prime Minister of the United Kingdom from 1979 until 1990. He was a business man. She is known as the Iron Lady and reduced government operations and spending. The greedy and corrupt union folks did not care for her.

"Those drug guys tore my new shirt and have that date with Tina tomorrow," Billy said.

"We will go to the mall after work and buy you the best shirt they have. I love you son. We will get through this together," John said.

"I love you too Uncle John. Thank you for everything," Billy said.

"Does this Tina look good? You are so lucky to be young and chasing the ladies," John said.

"Yeah, she has long black hair and nice calves," Billy said.

"Forget the calves. I have my own calves. I focus on the other qualities prized by the superficial male. Have you seen her mother?" John said.

John and Billy drive by the Hungarian Catholic Church in Frackville on the way home to Ashland. They see hundreds of immigrants in the woods under sheets draped between the trees. The Ministry of Interior dropped off 300 from the Mexican border this morning.

The government workers ran out of free housing and decided to dump them in rural America. There are crates of water bottles, dirty clothes on clothes lines, and piles of trash next to Highway 61. Most of them do not speak English and have only $100 that the border agents issued them.

"That is going to be a problem," John tells Billy sarcastically.

Most immigrants want to work hard and live the American dream, but there are not enough jobs. The stock market is down and people who worked hard and saved money are not feeling so successful anymore. Their taxes are going up every year and they are not investing in businesses.

The Ministry of Interior is dumping millions of immigrants all over the country. The government-controlled media cannot report on this operation. The local people must figure out how to deal with these illegal immigrants-newly minted citizens.

The immigrants live in the woods for five months. Urine and feces are everywhere and flowing into the yards in the neighborhood next door. Disease is spreading within the encampment and the local schools where the immigrants are learning English.

The Party officials come up with a solution. The police raid the Hungarian Catholic Church across from the encampment. They charge and arrest the priest and nun for sexual assault of a minor.

The charges are made up and the police plant evidence at the church. The Ministry of Interior confiscates the church and lets all 300 migrants move in. The migrants have four toilets to share.

"The essence of government is power and power lodged as it must be in human hands, will ever be liable to abuse," James Madison. (4)

The priest and nun are paraded on TV and sent to Site R. The reporter says horrible things about them. They are never heard from again. They ran the local church for thirty years together helping many poor folks in and around Frackville.

Meanwhile 900,000 protesters paralyzed Washington, DC today. They are very upset about the new value added tax put on all retail sales. The tax is 20% effective immediately.

The Party Ministry of Commerce based the tax on European countries. The European socialist and communists created this tax at 5% during the 1980s and then slowly raised it to 20% by 2000.

This VAT helped fun welfare and other free stuff for millions and millions of Europeans for decades. The high taxes reduced the will to work hard and pushed all the countries to socialism and weakness.

Russia and China took over parts of these European countries after they cut their military to the bone. They cannot defend themselves anymore.

The Democratic Socialist Party here skipped the teaser rate and jumped right to 20% right off the bat. Retail sales started decreasing immediately. Total tax revenue for government transfer payments and other programs is going down fast.

The government reports the day after the VAT protest that 698 anarchists were shot and killed when they attempted to shoot their way into the Congressional offices. Every protester had a pistol, rifle, or knife and fought to the death.

The organs of the dead protesters are removed by surgery at the George Washington University Hospital and put on ice in coolers. They are then flown to Party hospitals across the country. The hearts, livers, and lungs will save many Party members and their families. Only Democratic Socialist Party members are eligible for the organ transplants.

Life is less valued every year that goes by under the socialist government. It has been this way in the Middle East forever and now so it is in the US North. The Party is paramount and all citizens serve the Party's interests.

Sharon and John drive down to Cressona to visit her mother and John's sister living in the retirement home. The receptionist at the front desk tells them that she is not there.

They panic and ask many questions. They are afraid the Party took her away to Site R to punish their opposition.

"The government health care office in Reading came for her this morning. She needed an MRI on her knee after a fall," the political officer finally tells Sharon and John.

"This does not make sense. The nice nurse always calls me if she has any trouble. They are punishing us," Sharon said.

"I will tell you what. If they harm her in any way, somebody is going to see the end of my 9mm pistol," John said.

They rush to their car and drive to Reading to find Joan. The big potholes on Route 61 jerk the car left and right.

They see Joan in a wheelchair in the emergency room waiting area. She is in a great mood.

"Hey! How did you know I fell down and came down here?" Joan asks.

"We decided to visit you spur of the moment and you were not there!" Sharon said.

"How are you? Did they harass you?" John.

"No, no. Most of the employees are nice. I just fell down trying to dance again. A handsome man just moved in from Hummelstown," Joan said.

"I wonder why that nice nurse did not call me?" Sharon said.

"Oh, Julie was killed by the state security soldiers last week. She tried to prevent them from taking her aunt to Site R with a kitchen knife," Joan said.

"That is sick. These commies are so evil. Those Democrats and their soldiers will have a bad ending. Karma is for real," John said.

"I thought they were taking you to Site R. We know that the spies around Ashland know we are not thrilled with the socialism and government control of everything," Sharon said.

"So, did you have a good time dancing with the new guy on the block? Is he ugly or cute?" John said.

"Well we just started to dance and fell down. His teeth went flying and I broke my knee. He looked really different without the teeth. I cannot get that picture out of my mind," Joan said.

Joan, Sharon, and John drive up to the mall in St. Clair and have a great time. They push Joan in the wheelchair and enjoy the Chinese buffet.

A father and daughter walk into the mall when Joan and her family are coming out. The child sees an animal stuffed and hanging on the wall at the sporting goods store.

"Look, there is a camel!" the little girl screams at her dad.

"No, that is not a camel. That is a deer," the father corrects the excited and cute kid.

Two months ago more than 3,000 laborers died in Detroit after a fire engulfed a T-shirt factory where the workers worked and slept. Many died from smoke inhalation. Some died from impact after jumping out fourth-story windows.

The Party investigation revealed that the Democratic Socialist Party boss and her staff took bribes and kickbacks from the builder to cut safety standards. About $2 billion in cash, cars, and airplane trips changed hands.

The government executed 300 Party members by lethal injection. It was televised on national TV and millions tuned in for the punishment. The entire country and government is infected with corruption that came from government expanding so quickly.

At least the previous two-party system provided some checks and balances.

Many citizens squirmed in their recliners at home when many of the criminals died slowly on the tables. The Party had 300 tables with white linen sheets in a warehouse in Lansing for the TV show.

"Over grown military establishments are under any form of government inauspicious to liberty, and are to be regarded as particularly hostile to republican liberty," President George Washington. (4)

The doomed corrupt Party members were strapped to the tables like wild animals at a veterinary hospital. They were supposed to die quickly. Some were quiet and some yelled obscenities at the cameras. The government medical examiner experimented with the protocols and several mistakes were made. It took thirty minutes for some to stop moving and perish, but all were pronounced dead by 9:00 pm.

The execution show comes on just before the football game. The game gets a boost in viewership because of this timing.

Cyberattacks hit 200 cities this month. The government cannot protect its computer networks after reducing maintenance budgets for years. Party officials transferred the funds to pay for welfare and salary increases for union government workers. All government workers are in unions and they threaten to strike frequently. Phones and email are down in all the affected cities. The IT employees cannot determine when the services will be back online.

The Party officials cannot determine who is responsible. Most are corrupt and ignorant figureheads on the government payroll. The FBI is investigating and has not made any public statements.

Some cities lost their 911 system and 311 customer service system for weeks. Elderly citizens are dying alone. The bodies decay for days or weeks before anyone finds them.

Dale and Sharon are watching the news at night back in Ashland. The killings by the government and killings of government security personnel are increasing every quarter and every year since 2021.

"Suspected capitalist militants ambushed an Army convoy in Ohio today. The terrorists killed at least 230 brave socialist warriors in military vehicles. The bloodshed comes only weeks after the ambush of riot police in Denver at the downtown Arboretum. The deaths reported in that incident were 160 police and 350 protesters," handsome reporter with thick hair on the government run TV channel relays.

The attack in Denver occurred at night. The rebels had night vision goggles and most Army units do not. The Warner administration cuts the military budget every year to pay for social programs and interest on the national debt.

Millions of Americans must sell assets to pay their taxes. They sell houses, cars, boats, and more houses. This puts downward pressure on prices for everyone. This causes many jobs for uneducated people to disappear.

Chapter Four
Socialism Medium in 2023

President Warner is in a great mood. The date is January 10th, 2023. She spent most of last night at the White House pool with her harem. It consists of twenty men from Site R (the re-education complex in Pennsylvania).

The secret service agents select the most attractive and fit men for this official duty from prison. The President personally approves the men from a leather binder of pictures and biographies. The men are taken to the White House basement. They are examined for any disease at the Walter Reed National Military Medical Center.

The prisoners are not told that they will never emerge again from the White House basement. This is a lifetime government assignment and beyond top-secret. The good news for them is that the apartments are luxury and food divine.

Even the President's husband does not know about this pleasure operation. Only the President can enter the harem area. Chairman

Mao of China had the same type setup in the Forbidden City. The main difference is that he had a bunch of eunuchs around to care for the women in his harem. There is no need for eunuchs for this President.

President Warner loves to frolic with the harem men at the White House pool and think about JFK. He used to hang out at the pool with his girlfriends when Jackie was out of town.

President Clinton would have died for this harem setup. He could not get away with it due to the two-party system in effect at that time. He did have the Lolita Express and Epstein's Orgy Island available to him though.

The President's husband cries outside the White House pool room sometimes as he hears the men laughing and having a great time with his wife. She loves the attention, chemistry, and stimulation. Jackie used to cry in the same spot while listening to JFK have a great time in the pool with the other beauties.

President Warner is in the former United States Capitol Visitor Center in the huge bunker across the street from the Supreme Court this morning. The government leaders borrowed and built this monument to themselves back in 2008. They expanded it several times since then until the money ran out.

The President is here to rename the complex as the Great Hall of the People. All the top politicians are here. The House has been re-formed into the National People's Congress and enlarged from 435 fools to 4,000 fools.

The former Senate has been re-formed into the Politburo and enlarged from 100 Party members to 400 members. President Warner and her administration based the government organization loosely on the Chinese Communist Party.

"We are here to dedicate ourselves to the Democratic Socialist Party and our shared future. We have greatly improved our nation since the glorious election of 2020, but we have many challenges. We will not tolerate any dissent and use all means to ensure peace. Our socialism is the new era," President Warner said.

The speech lasts for three hours. The Party faithful give her many standing ovations. She has total power here. She has all the power Joseph Stalin had in 1922 to arrest, torture, and kill any dissidents.

"We have nationalized railroads, utilities, businesses, and universities together to make our country stronger. Our glorious socialist government has provided hundreds of thousands of nice homes taken from the filthy rich for our comrades. Let us now move forward together in solidarity," President Warner says to the massive adoring crowd.

The government leaders moved into the bunker because the US South and other enemy nations have nuclear weapons. Staff members and family members in The Party take over the old Capital Hill.

There was talk of war with US South after President Warner cut the water flow on the Mississippi River. The US South accuses Warner of behaving like the dictator of Sudan. He tries to cut the flow to the Nile River from time to time. The United Nations socialists facilitated talks to resolve the matter before any kinetic battles. The statistics, facts, and assumptions were manipulated to favor the north.

Sharon and Dale are lying in bed on this Friday night. They cannot watch TV because the only thing on is the National People's Congress coverage. The kids are in their rooms studying and listening to music. Dale had some candles lit before Sharon came upstairs.

The couple enjoys some erotica. Sharon thinks the candles are little silly. They are still in love and thank God for each other and this sanctuary from the socialist madness outside.

"I went to see Charlie today. It was horrible. He was emaciated and hunched over in the corner of his cell when I came in," Dale said.

"Really? That is terrible! "God help him," Sharon said.

Dale drove to Hamburg to see his old friend Charlie. He was caught drawing international attention to the mass incarcerations in Harrisburg and put in jail overnight without trial. This is commonplace now with The Party.

Amnesty International just included him on their prisoner of conscience list. This type of thing never happened in the old United States of America with limited government and three equal branches.

"The guards laugh at him and keep him in only underwear and a t-shirt in cold cells without shoes. They give him normal clothing when the rare visitor comes," Dale said.

"The Party is brutal. Those people do not like criticism. They are exactly like the Castro gang in Cuba," Sharon said.

"His wife is under house arrest. The beatings get worse when she tells anyone about the torture," Dale said.

"The government folks are going to burn in hell for this. I guess our fellow voters did not read about one-party rule and how disgusting it is," Sharon said.

"I agree! I only hope our socialists and communists do not last 70 years like the Mexicans, Russians, and Chinese did. I guess that is the world record for one-party rule in the modern age. I taught the kids about that last week," Dale said.

"His wife told me that the government accused him of being a paid spy for China. Now that is outrageous," Sharon said.

"You are a great father. Now come over here and satisfy me big daddy. And put out those dumb candles before you start a fire," Sharon said.

The next day Sharon takes Gina to an art show at Penn State University in Schuylkill Haven. The plan is to see the student art and then go out for a nice lunch.

When they pull up to the big parking lot on campus on Route 61 they see thousands of protesters. There are firebombs and burning tires all over.

"What is going on? I guess the art show is canceled," Gina jokes.

"Let us just sit over here and watch. This is how NOT to change government. I have never protested and believe that it is dumb," Sharon said. She thinks Gina can learn about the evils of socialism and communism by watching the anarchy a few minutes.

They sit in the car in front of the huge tattoo, piercing, and vaping superstore. This government-owned business has 3,000 locations and really took off after Congress passed the universal basic income law. Each store is the size of a Super Walmart.

The students are protesting a rise in fuel prices. They throw rocks at the big windows of the library. The government budget is tight and inflation is rising due to the US North dollar losing value.

The riot police walk slowly toward the students with body armor on and spraying tear gas. Many students have on gas masks, but the ones who do not are vomiting and choking.

"One man with a gun can control 100 without one," Vladimir Lenin. (4)

All of a sudden a student throws a Molotov cocktail onto the riot police. One officer screams from his arm burning. He runs to the medic vehicle for assistance.

A fat male student in sweatpants throws a javelin at the soldiers to the rear of the riot police. The javelin is a direct hit into the thigh of a soldier. He falls to the pavement and screams in agony.

The javelin thrower looks like a cross between an Olympic athlete and John Belushi. Except an Olympian would never be that overweight.

The snipers begin to shoot rubber bullets at the students. They are fed up with these violent kids. The gang of protesters disburses into the treeline and melt away avoiding arrest and sure torture.

"Wow! That was amazing! It is like that video game Fran had the other night," Gina said.

"Yeah I know. This is what you have with socialist one-party rule. This is what you have by coddling the youth with bullshit about socialism, victim-hood, and feelings. I hope and pray that you never get into the leftist, lazy bunch," Sharon said.

"Don't worry Mom. I have read enough history to know that capitalism and free enterprise are much better than socialism and communism. Let us get out of here," Gina said.

"Is that green light a laser beam? I think that man on the balcony is trying to blind the police," Sharon said.

"Yes, he has a laser pointer. That is the biggest and strongest one that I have ever seen," Gina said.

As they drive away Gina sees a student get hit in the eye with a rubber bullet. Blood is gushing everywhere and the female protester is in agony.

They drive up to Frackville and have a good country ham lunch at Cracker Barrel. They are so relieved that they were not walking around campus when the confrontation occurred.

"Mmm, Mmmmmm, this cornbread is awesome! Why don't more restaurants have cornbread?" Gina said.

"You are right. More restaurants should have cornbread," Sharon said.

Sharon hits a deep pothole on the way home to Ashland. The car swerves off the highway and almost hits the guardrail beside the marijuana dispensary. The drug people jump and run out of the way. There are always 10 or 20 hanging around outside at the gazebo spending their universal basic income.

The drug people live under the bridge on Highway 61 near the Dunkin Donuts in Pottsville in the summer. They lounge in old, nasty tractor trailer containers on the old golf course in the winter. The Democrat Party pays for everything and just tries to keep them from being violent or protesting.

The government workers had many extra shipping containers after the economy tanked. The golf course shut down when the communists took most of the assets of the wealthy.

The roads are getting worse and worse under the socialists. They are burning a lot of tax money on trying to keep the population appeased.

Sharon and Gina read in the local paper the next day that 214 students died in the protest. Ten riot police were injured. The government rules of engagement (ROE) allow deadly force in most situations.

Sharon and her co-worker are watching TV at the courthouse in Pottsville where they work. There was a huge explosion and fire five weeks ago in Allentown. The Pennsylvania regulator (Party Official) was supposed to oversee the local power company.

The government owns 70% of the utility and private citizens own 30%. The managers and regulators decided to cut the power line maintenance and safety budget every year for the last ten years. They took the $4 billion from the maintenance budget and spent it on climate change research conferences in California, windmills, and solar panels.

A transformer and power line blew up because of this lack of inspection and maintenance. The managers and Party officials inside the utility placed a higher priority on wild predictions of climate change and did not ensure the safety of the lines.

"The press should be not only a collective propagandist and collective agitator, but also a collective organizer of the masses," Vladimir Lenin. (4)

The Democratic Socialist Party officials in Harrisburg want to punish someone for the loss of 1,500 lives. The problem is that the Party officials inside and outside of the utility are to blame. The government leaders hide and destroy all evidence that points to Party criminals.

"The CEO and thirty other senior leaders of the Allentown Electric Company were hanged today for negligent homicide. Their actions caused the explosion and fire that killed 1,500 adults and children five weeks ago," the local reporter says on TV.

"That is amazing that no government fool was executed. You know they are at fault too," Sharon said.

"You bet that is true. The Party is scapegoating with the non-party idiots. Our government was never good with accountability, but it has gotten much worse," Kim said.

"It was discovered during the investigation by the Party that the utility leaders falsified forms submitted to the government," the reporter says.

"My friend in the utility told me that the government leaders made that up to transfer blame from the government to the private citizens. This lie supports the narrative for execution," Kim said.

The people in Allentown are having rolling blackouts since the explosion. The inept government workers ordered replacement parts from China, but it will take ten more weeks for the parts to arrive. Non-government utilities in other countries always have spare parts lying around.

Most days each house and business in the area only have power for 12 hours per day.

Allentown is like Basra, Iraq now. This lack of power was unheard of four years ago.

John is back at his auto parts store working at the front counter. His old friend Tony comes in for some oil.

"You will not believe what this guy told me last week. This is crazy stuff," Tony said.

"I will believe anything around here now. What are we going to do about these socialist bastards?" John asks.

"I do not know. This guy I met installed some drywall down in Hamburg at a top Party official's house. It is a mansion on 50 acres. The government took it from a rich business guy," Tony explains.

"I bet I know which one that is over behind the warehouses. It has pretty stone on the front and a four-car garage," John said.

"Yeah, that is it. My man walks by a trophy room on the way to the pool room he is working on. The door is slightly open and he see human heads and shoulders mounted on the walls!" Tony said.

"What? You just be kidding. Is that guy a liar?" John asks.

"No, no he was so disgusted and frightened by seeing that. What are these damn fools doing? It reminded him of that old movie The Hunger Games," Tony said.

"That Party official must be like Caligula. And I guess his family and friends are the same," John said.

"It is like we are in a bad movie. I cannot believe how brutal the one-party state is in such a short time period," Tony said.

"Yes, I guess these types of things happened under Saddam Hussein or Idi Amin," John said.

"The Butcher of Uganda! He was a jewel back in the 1970s. The commies in the Soviet Union supported that socialist fool. At least he kept the decapitated heads of his political enemies hidden in his freezer and not on the wall," Tony said.

"You know that communist Amin was a cannibal. He was a picky cannibal too. He complained about the humans tasting salty," John said.

"Seinfeld had a bit about that. He imagined waking up in the middle of the night worried about being eaten," Tony said.

"I would think that getting a good night's sleep would be the hardest thing about being a cannibal. Who is that? Who is there? Did you have dinner? I told you to eat something!" Jerry Seinfeld.

The Treasury Secretary is sad this morning. He thought he had a great idea to raise money to fund raises for all government people and more welfare, but he was wrong. The President and Secretary put 8% of the national oil company up for sale in an IPO on the New York Stock Exchange.

This company used to be known as Exxon, but the politicians took it over last year to generate cash for themselves. The target price was $10 per share, but investors were not impressed and stayed away from the sale. The shares went for only $2 per share.

The smart investors want a privately owned company that sells a great product or service, is efficient, makes a profit, and maximizes its stock price over the long term. They do not invest in companies owned by a socialist government with no internal controls to combat corruption.

A similar thing happened in Saudi Arabia back in 2019, except in that case at least the king could strongly encourage wealthy citizens to buy the stock of their national government oil company as a national duty. (8) The kingdom has 15,000 in the House of Saud (royal family) to feed and the unemployment rate for the young and chubby Saudis is high.

Fifty members of the Treasury staff are sent to Site R as punishment for this failed IPO.

Ten are hanged. The President continues to search for more tax money to feed the growing and corrupt government. She wants to stay in power a long time.

Meanwhile, production of oil and natural gas are going down. The Democratic Socialist Party members are sucking money out of the company for living expenses and to buy houses. The managers cannot maintain and repair the pipelines and other infrastructure.

The President and her socialist comrades talk more and more about climate change. They remain vague on the terms like what they mean by being "climate positive." Vague laws allow the government to convict, jail, and execute political opponents.

Environmentalists enjoy millions of great-paying government jobs and celebrate when business people or non-government people are punished. Rich and middle class citizens pay billions in taxes and fines for renewable energy projects. Much of the money goes directly to politicians and union government employees for pay, free health care, and free pensions.

The politicians and other government employees fly to conferences all around the world to talk about climate change. They try to agree on a definition for "recyclable" during the mornings and then knock off for facials and spa treatments during the afternoons. The government pays for everything.

The climate change crowd has vacationed on the government's dime for decades. The cannot seem to agree on targets to cut emissions or the details of a global carbon-trading system. The conferences will go on forever. The Party faithful from Hollywood and the District of Columbia love the winter meetings in southern France and summers in Switzerland.

The tax on financial transactions helps to fund the useless environmental conferences and vacations. Stocks and bonds decreased in value after this new tax was implemented last year. Al Gore would be shocked and proud of the progress. Socialism is great for the government people.

Chapter Five
Socialism Heavy in 2024

"The Interior Ministry official stated that three rockets landed in the vicinity of the White House last night. A secret service agent was killed on the East side of the building," the TV reporter relays on the nightly news.

"Boy, it is getting bad over here. I am glad that we do not live a big city," John says to his friend Tim. They were in the Army together.

"I know. It reminds me of when we were in Kuwait and the scuds came in. What a great time," Tim says joking around.

"Thirty protesters were killed in the rioting. Police and secret service agents opened fire with automatic machine guns in Lafayette Square," the news reporter relays.

"What the hell are these voters and socialists thinking? We almost beat that fool Warner in 2020. That is when this crap got really bad," John said.

"Fifty protesters were arrested and transported to the Hamburg, PA correctional facility. Several had life-threatening injuries," the TV reporter says.

"Did you see that puff piece on state TV last week? They said that the President gets ten thousand praise letters per week and that he answers all of them," Tim said.

"Yeah, I saw that crap. The dictators always do that. They pretend that the masses adore them. Mussolini claimed that he received and answered 1.8 million love letters back in the 1920s in Italy," John said.

"I guess that is how that fool staying in power for 23 years. Do you know that his daughter was a slut?" Tim said.

"No, I did not know that. That is awesome. Did she look good? A mob got rid of his stupid ass," John said.

"I wonder how many people work in the Ministry of Information. It has to be hundreds of thousands. They run it out of Hollywood," Tim said.

"That Hollywood bunch fit like a glove with the socialists when they grabbed power from Trump. They were promoting communism back in the 1940s," John said.

"I read that when the soldiers put an end to Ceausescu and his dumb wife they shot them in a freezing courtyard next to a toilet in 1989," Tim said.

"Yeah, I read that book "How to be a Dictator." (6) The funny thing is what Elena shouted at the firing squad just before they shot her," John says.

"Fuck You!" Elena Ceausescu screamed at her shooters.

"That communist idiot held power in Romania for 24 years. It is amazing how long these dictators last. They create a cult of personality just as they are doing here in the formerly great USA," Tim said.

"Remember what Nixon said about that cat? That was a good one," John said.

"He may be a commie, but he is our commie," Richard Nixon.

"Dumb and immoral Nixon messed up with the Chinese government folks. He did not see their threat to democracy and freedom by promoting socialism and communism all around the world. And so did Clinton by helping them get into the World Trade Organization. Chairman Mao and those communist bastards cheat on everything," Tim said.

"Yeah, you talk about a cult of personality. Mao was the best. I read that he had pillow fights with his harem every night in the Forbidden City. What a life," John said.

"Old Mao ruled for 27 years. What a man! He had the folks crying on demand at the dumb parades," Tim said.

"Boy, the Chinese people celebrated when he finally died. It looks like someone would have put him to sleep sooner," John said.

"I read that Stalin fired or killed many senior and experienced officers in the military and then suffered a few defeats. He got depressed and went to a secluded cabin. It seems like someone would have killed that sucker," Tim said.

"He lived a long time after that. He and his gang killed tens of millions of Soviets and others. Old FDR was a weak fool in dealing with Stalin. He let the Russians invade and take over six countries in 1939-1940," John said.

"I know, and he did not do a damn thing when the Russians slaughtered 22,000 poor Polish soldiers in 1940. Your man FDR was weak and stupid," Tim said.

"He is not my man. I think his wife was a lesbian. I do not blame her with that idiot in the house," John.

"Who was uglier Franklin or Eleanor?" Tim said.

"I think it is a tie. Both of the them could make a dog run up a tree," John said.

"You know I think our friends in the Democratic Socialist Party have studied and learned from the dictators. They seem to employ all their tactics to stay in power," Tim said.

"The purge took place yesterday. Two thousand senior officers and civilians were arrested and marched out of the Pentagon in handcuffs. The executions were performed at Fort Myers by firing squad. The weather was sunny and 40 degrees," the handsome reporter states on TV.

His hair is thick and his father is a senior Politburo member. The Party has 16 million members. They control the government and who gets all the good jobs. This goes for government jobs and business jobs. The government owns most businesses now.

"Social justice cannot be attained by violence. Violence kills what it intends to create," Pope John Paul II. (4)

Each company has several Party members on the board of directors, in management, and in all work groups. The Democratic Socialist Party must stay informed and on top of any rebellion. The collective socialist, communist is far more important than the individual in this society.

Dictators and dictator groups always enjoy the purge. This one was conducted because The Party suspected that the military people were planning a coup. Not much evidence is needed to conduct a coup nowadays. That leaves 30,000 people working at the Pentagon every day.

The Chinese government leaders helped set up US North a long time ago. They had plenty of experience keeping the folks down. Then it all blew up on them.

The American communists will not make the same mistakes of the Chinese communists. The Chinese government leaders tried not to make the same mistakes that the Russian government leaders made. The Russian communists fell in 1989.

All members of the military take an oath of office to the Democrat Party. They swear allegiance to back the socialists come what may. This is how it is done in China.

Furthermore, only Party members can join the military. You must demonstrate years of extreme devotion to The Party and/or the Dear Leader to be invited to join the Democrat Party.

All candidates for public office must be members of The Party. There are some elections, but no other political parties are tolerated.

Millions and millions of people are in prison. The communist party folks incarcerate them for practicing religion, protesting, killing others, selling goods without paying taxes, trying to escape to the nation of US South, and a thousand other reasons.

A LTC from Fort Belvoir and 400 of his soldiers died last week when they drove up to the White House for a visit. Their attempted coup was poorly planned and unsuccessful. The colonel was sick of having a Party official in his battalion overruling his decisions.

The Party officials are in every military unit nowadays and have ultimate authority. This ensures that the President can count on the support of the military.

The 401 deceased were cut to pieces by artillery and machine guns when they dismounted the vehicles at Lafayette Square. The LTC got the idea from reading about Hugo Chavez and wanted to be a hero for the capitalists. It took weeks to remove the blood and body parts from Pennsylvania Avenue and the north lawn.

The socialist Chavez led an unsuccessful coup d'etat against the president of Venezuela back in 1992. They put him in prison for two years and then made the mistake of pardoning him. He finally took over the government and proceeded to ruin the country with corrupt socialism for 14 long years. (5)

Dale and Michael are chatting at McDonalds restaurant one day over coffee. Their mutual friend has a son who was just shot down by the riot police in California. The son was at a massive protest in Los Angeles last week against one-party rule.

"I spoke with Pat yesterday at church. He is devastated. You will not believe what happened with his son. He was only 21 years old," Michael said.

"Did soldiers return the body to Pat at his house in Port Carbon?" Dale asks.

"Yes they did. The older officer demanded that Pat pay $10,000 cash and admit in public that his dead son was a member of a violent militia that tried to overthrow the government. He would only get the body if he agreed to those terms," Michael said.

"That is disgusting. Can you believe that our government people are acting like the mafia? This makes me so mad" Dale said.

"The Army officers also told Pat that if he told anyone about the terms he would be jailed and tortured," Michael said.

"That is hideous. I will not tell anyone to protect Pat. God help him. I read that the Iranian government has been doing stuff like this for years," Dale said.

"Let us drop off some good food tonight for Pat and the wife and kids. We need a revolution, but how can we get weapons?" Michael asks.

"Okay. Surely some of the socialists and communists regret voting this evil gang into office. The Party's behavior is so evil, but I cannot imagine how anyone would overthrow this regime," Dale said.

"Pat told me that the creeps who brought his son's body had another body in the huge, black SUV. They wanted to know the best way to Shenandoah," Michael said.

"Who are these people? The Sopranos? I guess they would dump the body in the Susquehanna River if he did not pay up," Dale said.

"This is like living in North Korea or Cuba. Or perhaps living in Nazi Germany back in the 1930s," Michael said.

"I need to remind my kids to never, ever be around protests. This is not like the anti-war protests against Operation Iraqi Freedom for sure," Dale said.

"Fidel Castro would be proud of this group. I heard that the communists down there in Cuba really excel at torture," Michael said.

"Yes they do. I guess the mental torture hurts as much as the physical torture and the government folks know that," Dale said.

"The North Koreans used to put Americans in water cages up to their necks and let rats bite them over and over, Michael said.

"Let us pray that this too shall pass," Dale said.

"What is going on at your hospital?" Michael asks.

"Well, do you remember when the Obama regime spoke of rationed care? They tried to keep it a secret, but word got out about the death panels," Dale said.

"Yes, that was about 2010 and the whole Obama Care stuff sounded so dumb. Why would you want government fools to provide your healthcare? The cannot even pave the roads," Michael said.

"I treated Mrs. Woods for years and years and helped manage her disease. You remember her from Hazleton? She was doing fine until last month," Dale said.

"I remember her well. She volunteered at my daughter's school for years as a math tutor," Michael said.

"Last month a Party official walked into my office without an appointment or prior notice. He said that Mrs. Woods has been transferred to Site R for end-of-life care," Dale said.

"My friend told me about Site R. They have thousands of sick and old people out there. It is very unsanitary and people do not last long. They even deposit healthy people there who just argue with the government employees," Michael said.

Site R is a top-secret government complex in Pennsylvania deep inside a mountain. It was built during the 1950s to house the President, other top federal politicians, and their families in the event of nuclear war.

"Ideas are more powerful than guns. We would not let our enemies have guns, why should we let them have ideas," Joseph Stalin. (4)

There are restaurants, grocery stores, huge water tanks and wells in tunnels. The tunnels go on for miles and miles. Over the years the government workers expanded Site R to include several massive re-education camps and prisons. The capacity is two million prisoners in tremendous warehouses and fenced-in areas.

"You are right on that one. She died this week. I received an email death notice. She could have lived years if the government had just let me do my job. The guy was proud about the tax money saved," Dale said.

"Wow, these communist are brutal. Does that type thing happen often with your patients?" Michael said.

"They sentence about ten patients per month to Site R per doctor at my place! God help us all," Dale said.

Sharon is back in Ashland at the high school. Gina and the history teacher got into another argument in class. Sharon must meet with the principal, teacher, and Gina to work things out.

The Democratic Socialist Party controls all education in the country. This includes K though 12th and college. Much of the curriculum consists of ideas laundered through universities for decades. There are many assumptions, opinions, and feelings in the teaching plans. The teachers must state opinion as fact.

The principal and all teachers are Party members. They will never deviate from the propaganda they are given for the students.

Their punishment will be prison, torture, or death if caught poisoning the minds of the youth.

"Gina insists on arguing about climate change. She tells the other students that the Earth goes through cooling and heating phases and that is normal," the teacher says.

"Well, that is true. We know that mankind pollutes, but what she said it true. And why do you teach that gender is all in your mind? That is bullshit and not a biological fact," Sharon said.

"Can you just keep quiet in class? We do not want you affecting the other students," the principal asks Gina.

"Gina disputes my lectures about the former USA being largely racist and unsuccessful," the teacher said.

"That is very misleading and inaccurate. A small minority of Americans were racist. The former USA was the most successful nation to ever exist on this planet," Sharon said.

"Can you just remain quiet if you disagree with anything your teacher says?" the principal asks Gina.

The conference discussion proceeds like this for hours. Sharon corrects the teacher on point after point. The teacher is teaching propaganda and not facts or science.

Sharon is smart enough to realize not to challenge the Party representatives running this high school. They alone can commit Sharon and Gina or anyone to Site R or other re-education facilities. The Party officials are smart enough to realize that they need Dale as a doctor in this village for their own children.

Gina finally agrees to just be silent when she disagrees with her teachers. She is stubborn like her parents and distinguishes between fact and assumption as all intelligent and educated people do.

This educational program is indoctrination and not true education. The schools were politicized many years ago. The Party members must spin all facts and assumptions past and present.

Sharon and Gina walk out of the principal's office, down the hall, and out to the car. Sharon is worried that her daughter will challenge the lies from the teacher and get sent to Site R.

"You are correct on every dispute with the propaganda-spreading teacher. But please just be quiet and do not argue with this dolt. They can really hurt us," Sharon said.

"I know and will try to keep quiet. It is just so hard to sit there while the government teacher lies and says dumb stuff all the time.

Most of the students just believe her," Gina said.

"Thank you. I am so proud of you and we will escape this communist paradise soon. Your father and I are working on a plan. Do not tell anyone," Sharon said.

"Of course, that is top-secret. Thank goodness you saved all those real textbooks and hid them in the basement. The schools used to really educate kids," Gina said.

Gina is surrounded by teenagers suffering from anxiety and depression. Suicide rates are increasing. Government people and the politicians causes much of this.

Government leaders have been making fun of Christians and Biblical values since the Obama regime was elected during 2008. Obama and others demoted religion and promoted government programs to increase dependency. They did this despite the fact that kids in a Christian home have lower rates of mental problems and crime.

"The best argument against democracy is a five-minute conversation with the average voter," Winston Churchill. (4)

The world population is 80% religious, but the Obama folks rejected them and promoted things like gay marriage. Most foreigners saw a US government recklessly spending the nation into ruin and preaching odd social values.

Most Americans have always believed in equal rights for all. But most do not believe in promoting lifestyles that lead to self harm over others. The Bible creates boundaries between right and wrong. Boundaries are great for children.

The textbooks and internet were scrubbed by communist censors years ago. It is difficult to find anything critical of the Democratic Socialist Party or its propaganda. There are hundreds of thousands censors working full-time government jobs now policing the internet for inconvenient truths.

"There has never been a democracy with ignorant citizens and there never will be," Thomas Jefferson.

Sharon and Gina drive past Gordon Mountain on the way back home in Ashland. It is a huge mountain with beautiful trees as far as the eye can see. Sharon sees smoke coming from the Smith compound and just smiles. She never mentions the rebel camp to Gina or Billy.

There are thousands of pockets of resistance across the country. The rebels are not pleased with the direction of the country. They plot for revolution to allow for the restoration of capitalism. The plot to escape the country and settle in US South if revolution is impossible.

Life expectancy was 76 for a man and 81 for a woman in 2020. Now it is only 72 for a man and 75 for a woman. Medicare for All provides poor and slow health care. Many expert doctors and nurses left the unstable country.

Democratic Socialist Party officials and their families get the best health care from military hospitals and clinics. The military medical equipment is handed down to non-party hospitals after a few years of use.

Somewhere in California an old couple is walking on the beach. They see a huge pipeline draining raw garbage into the sea. The tide is out and uncovers this top-secret government operation.

EPA Administrator AOZ has helped shut down most of the nuclear power plants in the name of climate change. The problem is not enough capacity to run sewage plants or anything. Blackouts are common now in every province.

The socialists ignored or forgot about the Germans doing the same thing from 2011 until 2022. Their citizens have suffered with high electricity prices and blackouts for 13 years now. The US North people are just beginning to suffer the consequences of the bad decisions of the socialists and communists running the government.

The Germans lost a lot of wealth and power from their dumb climate change policies and now the American socialists are doing the same. The Audi CEO only spent a little time in prison during 2018 for lying about how good diesel is for the environment. Chancellor Merkel avoided jail for her part in the diesel propaganda and testing scam.

The windmills and solar panel fields are working, but cannot replace the capacity of the now-idle nuclear power plants. The average temperature has gone down in the last few years in this new country.

The National Oceanic and Atmospheric Administration has two million full-time government employees writing report cards on 200 countries. But they cannot seem to find the time to write a report card on themselves. They do enjoy high salaries, free health care, free pensions, and other great benefits.

"Socialism is a philosophy of failure, the creed of ignorance, and the gospel of envy, its inherent virtue is the equal sharing of misery," Winston Churchill. (4)

The Earth is about 4.5 billion years old and has gone through climate change many times. The last ice age ended about 13,000 years ago. The ice melted and the oceans rose and many places were separated by water such as Australia and New Guinea. The humans can and should reduce pollution, but cannot control Earth or the weather.

AOZ hired Jeremy Corbyn from the United Kingdom after he got thrown out of the government over there in 2019. The British voters were sick and tired of the socialists and communists creeping into government and trying to kill the free enterprise system.

The funny thing was that AOZ endorsed and supported the socialist Corbyn and company in their election. They bonded over antisemitism and big and corrupt government.

"Under our leadership, we will remove all resistance to authority involving environmental matters. The capitalist polluters must pay a price for ruining the environment," the Assistant EPA Administrator Corbyn says to the crowd.

"Everybody is going to save the planet. Are they kidding me? We do not even know how to take care of ourselves. The planet is fine. Humans have only been here for 300k years and the planet 4.5 billion years. The planet will be here long after the humans become extinct," George Carlin.

Jeremy Corbyn is so dedicated to his union money that he once missed his son's birth because he was giving a speech to some union members. The birth and speech were in the same hospital. (5) Now that is dedication to the socialist union cause.

"We reversed the navigable water rule under our leadership. Now we regulate a lot more of America than Obama or Trump ever did," AOZ brags to the faithful.

Obama and his EPA folks took over more land by saying that puddles and tiny pools of water are navigable for boats and ships. Trump reversed this abuse. Warner and AOZ reversed Trump. Warner takes Obama's regulatory abuse and harassment of business owners to another level.

Most government employees have free generators for their offices and houses. They never have the blackouts that non-party members go through every week in their homes. The Party must have power 24/7 to run the country and enjoy a fabulous lifestyle. The generators run on diesel fuel and are hidden from view.

At 6:30 in the morning on a lazy Thursday in the Treasury Secretary's office in

Washington, DC a tragedy unfolds. The Secretary is found dead from an overdose of opioids. He grabbed a bottle of his son's drugs and took them to work. The son just received a free 120-day supply.

He has been lying about the country's finances for four years now and the pressure caught up with him. The assistant found his body on the floor behind the huge mahogany desk in the office suite.

He and his team just negotiated their way out of a jam. They could not come up with $800 billion for a Treasury bond payment. The former United States and this new country known as US North have never defaulted on debt in 248 years. He did not want to be responsible for defaulting now.

The Secretary's father was a Democrat governor of a corrupt Democrat state a while back and a life-long sleazy Democrat. His dying wish to President Warner was to make his son the Treasury Secretary. The governor gave millions to the campaign to increase his odds and that helped.

The newly deceased Secretary always made a lot of money with jobs in the Democrat Party and was not too bright. He was a big drinker and started thinking about his children. They would not have a country if he continued to help the White House lie, tax, and spend. His wife is not concerned with such things and just really enjoys the fortune and fame.

The IMF and World Bank socialists in collaboration with the American socialists worked a deal to extend the maturity of the debt from 30 years to 100 years to lower the debt and interest payments. They proclaim that technically this is not a default.

"Nothing in all the world is more dangerous than sincere ignorance and conscientious stupidity," Martin Luther King, Jr. (4)

The Secretary managed to hide all this from the public and international investors. The media cannot report on this story. It would have been embarrassing for President Warner to default after only four years in power. She nominates and the Senate quickly confirms Beto Oneal from Texas as the next Treasury Secretary.

He is only 52 and full of energy for socialism and more government. He always does his best for the drug dealers, criminals, people who refuse to work, people who refuse to pay their debts, climate-change snake oil salesmen, violent Muslims, illegal immigrants, and gun control nuts. He will fit right in at the cabinet meetings. He will enjoy free conference trips on big government airplanes to Hawaii and Switzerland with his staff and family.

Many dams across the nation are decaying and failing. Each failure kills many citizens. The government cuts the inspection and regulatory budget of the Mine Safety and Health Administration every year. The funds are transferred to pay for Medicaid, food stamps, free housing, college tuition, and many other welfare programs.

Most dams go without inspections for years. The government owns 90% the dams, but keep business people involved with 10% ownership. This is just enough to blame them when bad things happen. The Party executes many business people after each dam failure.

Sometimes government leaders take bribes to protect the dam owners and managers. They are executed in public for failure to follow Party discipline. The Socialist Democratic Party is supreme and cannot be held accountable for infrastructure or any unnecessary deaths or injuries.

The manager of the Hoover Dam was hanged in public when his dam failed. He embezzled millions of dollars from the budget to repair drainage problems. The water built up inside the dam and finally gushed out killing many in its path. This manager was a top tier Democratic Socialist Party member and had four houses in four countries.

Chapter Six
The 2025 American Police State

President Warner and her team have steadily eroded confidence in the economy, weakened democratic institutions, and perverted the Federal Election Commission for the last four years. They have nationalized or taken control of millions of businesses by placing Party officials on the boards and/or in management. She is proud of the march to socialism and believes things will get better. She is wrong.

The Ministry of the Interior announced that the re-education camps across the nation are needed for job training and to combat terrorism. The government leaders rarely speak about these facilities, but had to respond to criticism coming from the United Nations and Europe.

This situation is similar to China's treatment of Muslims back during 2018. China put about one million in re-education prisons and Muslims from other countries began to complain. The Muslims wanted political and religious freedom and China just told everyone that they were terrorists.

The US North government is embarking on a massive media campaign now to shape world opinion. The White House has allies at the UN and other global organizations saying things like "There is a problem with extremism and they are taking care of it."

The socialists inside US North and out agree to hide the fact that most people in the camps are political dissidents and sick people. They are sent there to die and save tax money spent on health care.

The expanded IRS has seized many assets from innocent citizens and businesses and sold them. This helps fund many government programs and lavish lifestyles for Party members.

The National Security Council and Pentagon leaders have taken the President's orders and ran with them. Now there are political staff officers or Party officials on staff at all brigade and higher headquarters in the Army, Navy, Air Force, Marines, and Coast Guard. The White House has many eyes and ears now to push propaganda and detect and jail rebels.

Joe Smith was in the Army for thirty years a while back before America split into two nations. He and his wife own 50 acres and raise and sell corn and soybeans. They used to raise cows, but the government shut that down because they believe in man-made beef only.

There are 400 local people living in Joe's barns. The government does not know about this group. They oppose the communist government and plan for revolution.

The capitalist radicals are lucky in one respect. The Ministry of Agriculture is run out of Washington, DC by bureaucrats and Party members who have never set foot on a farm. They would not know a farm if they tripped over one. They think all farmers are stupid and only good for raising taxes for the government folks to enjoy spending.

The main barn is massive measuring 200 feet by 150 feet. It has two stories and looks rough on the outside to disguise what is inside.

It appears to have only farm equipment downstairs and old wood, fertilizer, and supplies upstairs. But hidden between the supplies are nice apartments for all the residents. Boxes of ammunition are hidden in the floors.

They have piles and piles of water bottles, blankets, eggs, spam, tents, pistols, rifles, cooking oil, crossbows, and everything an army could want.

Joe and his wife Kathy taught the youngsters how to make Molotov cocktails. There are 2,000 stacked neatly in the corner of an apartment. The Party would execute everyone here if they discovered this war effort.

Sharon and Dale know Joe and Kathy and support them with funds and free medical care. But Sharon and Dale keep the operation from their kids to protect them. They dream of the day for revolution or escaping from this socialist or communist paradise.

The last time the Party official dropped by Dale's medical office he asked about Sharon's mother. He made a veiled threat about sending her to Site R if they went against the Party.

The socialist knows somehow that Dale and his family are not thrilled about the direction of the country. Perhaps he just knows about Gina arguing at school, but Dale is not sure how much he knows.

"It's easier to run for office than to run the office," Thomas O'Neill. (4)

Joe and his gang of farmers loved the former United States of America. They loved limited government and freedom for the individual and capitalism. They desperately want to overthrow the communists and/or escape to the south with some of their treasures. They firmly believe in The Bible and God and Jesus.

Joe and Kathy are talking with the others in the big barn. Their capitalists are mostly young adults with some older people.

"What happened over on Blue Mountain last year? We have heard different things," the farm worker asks Joe.

"It is a very sad tale. Tim and Patty were a lot like Kathy and I. They owned 100 acres and raised cattle and corn. After the Trump gang were run out of office, they started a resistance force just like us," Joe explains.

"They had about a thousand freedom fighters in several big barns and a very nice fence around the farm. The government found out what they were up to," Kathy said.

"The Democratic Socialist Party and army invaded on a Sunday during church services at the farm. They killed all 986 rebels," Joe said.

"We saw the pictures from the hunting camera next to the barn. It transmitted pictures to us. Thousands of soldiers walked around the farm shooting and killing everyone. The soldiers where smiling and laughing in the pictures. Nobody survived," Kathy said.

"That is why we cannot get too big here. There are hundreds of the pockets of resistance in the country, but it is almost impossible to coordinate and overthrow the socialists/communists," Joe said.

"We need to just keep at it and one day hopefully we can rise up and take the country back," Kathy said.

It took Nebuchadnezzar thirteen years to destroy the city of Tyre about 2,600 years ago. It finally fell. The Democrat Party's army only took two days to destroy the Blue Mountain freedom fighter's city.

A couple months ago the Party security personnel brought a man to Dale for emergency medical treatment. The man was 30 years old and had lacerations on his arms and legs. He was from Site R.

One guard stayed by his side for most of the visit to treat an infection. Dale was alone with the prisoner for about five minutes when the guard walked outside to smoke a joint.

"We must get out of here doctor. They are going to kill everyone. They strapped me to the wall for two days this week. Please help us," the prisoner said.

"Okay, we are making plans. Hang in there. God bless you. Just try to get along and do not make waves," Dale said.

"Yes doctor, but they made us watch a pit bull attack and kill four old women last week. These socialists are pieces of shit! Please break us out. Can you take some food to my father?" the prisoner asks.

"Certainly, just give me his name and address and we will help him. Do not worry about that," Dale said.

The guard walks back into the exam room and takes the prisoner away. He grabs some rubber gloves and scissors on the way out the door.

"Employ your time in improving yourself by other men's writings, so that you shall gain easily what others have labored hard for," Socrates. (4)

Dale knows that the Party guards are the worst of the worst. They dress in all black. There is no written exam to join and no moral training for the guards or the leaders. This setup is directly from the Nazi army setup in the 1930s.

The Party only wants uneducated young guards who will do anything required for absolute control. They will follow any order and not question whether it is moral or not.

Hitler would be proud of these men and women.

There are at least two rows of guards when they charge at protesting radicals to arrest or kill them. The first row takes care of business. The second row executes any guard in the first row who hesitates when following orders. The Party leadership learned this from the Iraqis during Operation Iraqi Freedom (OIF) in 2003.

The government minders and soldiers pull up at the Frackville hotel in a big, black SUV. They are coming to escort Jane and Tom, the visiting journalists from North Korea, to the festival at the edge of town. Two soldiers dressed in all black are sitting in the back of the vehicle and pointing a huge machine gun out the back.

The foreign and domestic media are tightly controlled in this country. The Democratic Socialist Party approves and controls all media content from its IT department in Hollywood, CA. The Americans spent time in North Korea observing government operations beginning in 2021 and the two nations are allies now.

They drive down Main Street and see a former doctor's office shut down. The sign taped on the cracked window reads "Not Fit for Human Habitation." There is not much tax money for health care around here. The sun is going down during their drive to the stadium.

The Ministry of Health Affairs is constantly looking for ways to reduce the population. They encourage and force many women to have abortions. Active euthanasia is used at re-education camps across the country.

They drive on the pothole-riddled streets. There is asphalt patch upon asphalt patch and orange circles around old potholes that were never filled. Workers long ago marked the holes, but never came back to fill them.

The buildings on Main Street are dilapidated with fungus on the faded awnings. The sidewalks are cracked and unsafe. The place looks like Haiti or Bangladesh. Many windows have duct tape and faded paint on them. Business has withered and died here.

The journalists see a small car on fire and stuck in a brick building. An opioid addict just crossed the center line and crashed into a vaping store. Four customers and the driver are dead. This happens all day every day across the drug-addicted nation.

Addiction rates skyrocketed after the politicians started paying a universal basic income. Many people could not handle the freedom of being unemployed with cash.

The bricks are cracked and the mortar is falling onto the sidewalks. The steel outside the buildings is rusted. Many retail spaces are empty. There is little hope here anymore.

They drive down a gravel and dirt road two miles. The driver parks at the edge of a big field and the three government workers and two journalists walk to the grandstands. The crowd is large and loud.

"Bohemian Rhapsody" by Queen is blasting on the speakers on telephone poles. The North Koreans are surprised with the loud music and do not know what to expect.

A large pen with 400 warthogs in it is next to the stadium. The government operation brings in a lot of money with exports. The money is badly needed for schools, prisons, and roads.

There are metal detectors and retina scanners at the entrance. The Party officials greet the North Koreans and escort them to the front row. Some government journalists in attendance met them years before in North Korea and enjoy catching up. All citizens sat for retina scans and fingerprints back in 2021.

The walkway into the stadium is lined with a tall fence on both sides and about twenty feet wide. There are large flags on poles with esteemed socialist and communist leaders on them. "Walk of Heroes: Socialism and Communism Forever!" is engraved on the arch.

"Don't Fear The Reaper" blares from all the speakers. Blue Oyster Cult sang about the inevitability of death in this classic rock song. The old DJ loves this music and thinks the crowd will respond to it today.

There are big flags for Idi Amin, Mao Zedong, Alexandria Ocasio-Cortez, Joseph Stalin, Pete Seeger, Beth Warner, Fidel Castro, Robert Owen, Karl Marx, Barack Obama, Joe Biden, Hillary Clinton, John Brennan, Ruth Bader Ginsburg, Frederich Engels, Kim Jong-un, Vladimir Lenin, Elizabeth Warren, Tony Benn, Leon Trotsky, Che Guevara, Bernie Sanders, Mikhail Gorbachev, Jeremy Corbyn, and others.

The mandatory event is held in a former high school football stadium. The old Party official in the infield control tower is the acting DJ and playing rock and roll. He plays the Rolling Stones song "You Can't Always Get What You Want."

There are laser light shows going on and most people seem to be enjoying themselves. The stadium capacity is 7,100 and it is almost full tonight. There are hundreds of soldiers roaming around carrying loaded rifles and occupying the four guard towers surrounding the stadium.

A thick red rope surrounds the seats for the Democratic Socialist Party officials, their families, and friends. Jane and Tom and their group sit in the crowded bleachers. The DJ plays some Pete Seeger communist protest music.

There are a few food stands next to the grandstands selling hot dogs, hamburgers, coffee, candy apples, and candy. Many people are quiet and crying. Many people are having a good time and joking about how the world is upside down in the former United States of America.

The Democratic Socialist Party members are in a good mood on this clear night. They are discussing how much tax money it will save the local chapter by terminating these criminals. Many of the them have been in prison for a while and costing a fortune.

The government, Party, and union folks eat and visit with each other. They are very happy to be on the correct side of politics and safe. They never liked the redneck conservatives, business people, Christians, or Republicans anyway.

"The first group tonight were caught selling corn and tomatoes outside the government market. They pocketed tax money as if it was their own. They also had several Trump-Pence 2020 campaign flags on their walls. These capitalist pig rednecks must die!" the announcer yells on big speakers that are everywhere.

He is so excited to destroy any opponents of his socialist government. The twenty unlucky capitalists have their hands bound behind their backs. They are led by the guards up a metal walkway above a bonfire. One by one the executioners place hoods on their heads. The criminals are then pushed into the fire to their death.

The criminals can request their walk on song for their execution. They also may choose their last meal from a limited menu. The DJ plays "Slow Ride" by Foghat and "Tight Rope" by Stevie Ray Vaughn to get the party started.

The crowd members who know the criminals are mostly successful in celebrating their lives tonight. What other choice do they have? Attendance at these events is mandatory. Death should come quickly in the fire.

The townsfolk cheer for the entertainment. Four years of being told that The Party is more important than the individual will change a soul. They cheer and are so glad inside that their loved ones or themselves are not being sacrificed to the gods of communism.

The DJ plays "Light My Fire." He put a lot of thought into the music selection and lyrics. The crowd loves the old rock and roll songs. Many of the executed are real criminals, but many just love capitalism and want the former free enterprise United States of America back.

Many criminals are sick of the brutal socialist rulers and have led protests and assassinations. They have lost the will to live under evil politicians and party members. The song from the Beatles "Taxman" blares from all the speakers within and outside the stadium.

"The second group tonight were caught stealing opioids from the Health Ministry. They had a good time and now we have a good time!" the announcer exclaims.

The group of twenty drug addicts and drug dealers are led up the walkway and pushed into the raging fire. The crowd cheers and are glad that the addicts will not strain government resources anymore.

The DJ plays "I Want a New Drug" by Huey Lewis and the News. The DJ tries to pick songs that fit the crime if he can. He tries to make the event fun and a celebration of life in a twisted way.

"One of the penalties for refusing to participate in politics is that you end up being governed by your inferiors," Plato. (4) That is an understatement.

The Democratic Socialist Party leaders used to be nice and give billions to the drug addicts and dealers in exchange for votes. They used to let the dealers off on probation and short sentences. The leftist politicians used to blame a lot of things on racism. The Party does not need their votes anymore.

"The third group we have here tonight were arrested while drinking illegal whiskey in a garage with a US South flag hanging on the wall. These twenty traitors admitted their loyalty to the enemy nation to our south and its capitalist ideals! The police also found urine-stained Obama-Biden 2008 campaign flags on the floor. They kept tax money from the government and the people," the announcer lets everyone know.

The DJ plays "Gimmie Back My Bullets" by Lynyrd Skynyrd. Ronnie Van Zant sings about consuming too much whiskey in the song.

The final group for tonight are corrupt Party officials. The opportunity for bribes is great when dealing with life and death of non-party citizens. Many Party officials will bend or break rules and laws for the right price. Families will pay anything to keep their loved ones out of prison.

"These high Party officials violated their oath to faithfully fulfill the sacred mission of workers in socialism for the Democratic Socialist Party. They have dishonored the leadership and spit on the motherland! Tonight their punishment is here!" the DJ announces.

"I hope they cook this meat well done," one old lady whispers to her husband in the crowd. The crowd roars with approval. This is the most popular part of the execution program. The non-party folks love to see the corrupt and evil Party members perish. The rednecks are going crazy.

"Me too, he is the jerk who took the money, but did not save Billy from going to prison. I saw Clara in Gordon last week and she is so lonely without Billy. I hope that commie bastard burns in hell," the husband replies.

The DJ plays "I Got Friends in Low Places" by Garth Brooks. The crowd goes wild and has a wonderful time. Many are drunk or high on drugs and enjoy the ultimate reality show. Admission is free.

"That was a hell of a show! The corrupt lady they fried from the tax office looked very nice. I was going to ask her out. She had nice calves," John said.

"You are crazy. I remember when we used to watch the kids play football here. Let us adjourn for a milkshake at that place in Ashland," Pat said.

"Yes, perhaps that new Party Chairwoman will be there. She is beautiful. I met her the other day. Let us go talk some trash," John said.

After all the festivities and killings, Jane and Tom are escorted back to the SUV for the trip back to the government hotel in Frackville. They see a sign at the edge of the field next to the dirt parking lot. It reads "Burning of the addicts and criminals every first and third Wednesday of the month. All citizens must attend."

A Democratic Socialist Party official runs after the North Koreans and catches up to them and their guards in the parking lot.

"Hey, you two are invited to the Party dinner starting right now. Are you hungry? Come with me! That includes you too," the young official tells the Koreans and the guards.

The DJ plays "Communication Breakdown" by Led Zeppelin as the crowd disperses to take it on home. The Party officials, families, and friends stay in place to enjoy steak, shrimp, wine, and cheese. The government pays for everything as a reward for being good socialists and saving tax money.

"I think the mass executions here are more festive than at home. We can make some improvements when we get back. Our events are too short and serious," one North Korean says to the other.

"Yes, I liked the music, snacks, criminal background information, and insults very much. We will share this information with the Dear Leader," one North Korean to the other.

Later back at the hotel, the Koreans discuss the events of the evening. They are impressed with how well the Party officials live here. They are in the Communist Party at home, but only have basic food. They eat mainly rice and sometimes have hamburger meat.

comrades so they can enjoy a nice life and retirement. Perhaps they can now take a trip to Disney World every year," President Warner brags.

Dale and Billy are waiting in Lafayette Square across the street from the White House for the parade to begin. The father makes sure they are far away from the government surveillance cameras and listening devices on all the light poles.

"This must be one of Dante's levels of hell to see AOZ, Sandman, Oneal, and all the other nitwits in the cabinet on TV every night bragging about stupid and wasteful government programs," Dale said.

Dante Alighieri wrote The Divine Comedy in the 1300s which described nine concentric circles of torment in hell. Each circle represents a gradual increase of wickedness. (5)

"That AOZ says some pretty funny things. She reminds me of a girl in my class who is beyond ignorant. She thought brown cows produce chocolate or brown milk," Billy said.

There are 90 million security cameras in the country today. The Party knows that pockets of resistance are growing. The capitalist rats must be identified and exterminated in this socialist paradise.

Dale is still thinking about the brutal end to the FDA Administrator yesterday. Some business owners bribed him to approve cheap baby formula in a streamlined way. The government-controlled corporation's toxic baby formula hit the market two weeks ago. It killed 5,600 babies across the country on the first day of sales.

"When you see a rattlesnake poised to strike, you do not wait until he has struck to crush him," Franklin D. Roosevelt. (4)

FDR used the IRS to punish newspaper owners for criticizing him and his dumb policies. Socialists like FDR always turn out to be dictators and control freaks. They must try to control the masses to stay in power.

The White House charged the FDA guy and 200 business men and women with murder directly at the Supreme Court. They were shot by firing squad yesterday at Fort Meade. Things get done quickly in communist countries like here and China.

The crooked FDA leader was in the Politburo and he embarrassed the Party very much. He had to be executed and fast to set an example.

This ceremony is special in celebrating four years of socialism and the defeat of capitalism and the three equal branches of government of the former United States of America. Only 10% of Americans are allowed or invited to join the Democratic Socialist Party (about the same as in China with their Communist Party). China sent thousands of advisers to help devise the new government in 2020, just as Russia had done for China in 1949.

There is a 40 by 30 foot portrait of the Dear Leader Warner hanging on the Old Executive building next to the White House. She was elected back in 2020 by promising free stuff to all American citizens and illegal immigrants. The cult of personality began at this time with the new regime. She also promised that all citizens would make about the same amount of money regardless of effort and education.

Soon after being sworn in, she brought the Supreme Court, House, and Senate under party control. Three branches were just too many. Two political parties were just too many and could not be controlled from the District of Columbia.

Millions of citizens were sent to re-education prisons and/or exterminated. Millions of Americans with money and nice houses took what little they could and fled to other countries. The government confiscated most of their wealth that they had worked decades for. The government office in Hollywood took over all media and employs tens of thousands of censors.

The nation's finances are more dire than the public realizes. Transparency went out the window after the election of 2020. International investors will not buy President Warner's bonds anymore.

"Can you help me review for my history test tomorrow?" Billy asks his father Dale.

"Sure, remember that US soldiers take an oath of office to the Democratic Socialist Party and The Dear Leader when they join the Army. Before 2021 they took an oath of office to the US Constitution. It mandated three equal branches of government, small and limited government, equal rights for all, freedom of speech, the right to bear arms, and freedom of religion," Dale explains.

"The old system sounds a lot better than the new system. Small government is always going to allow for more individual freedom and happiness. It also will save a ton of tax money from waste and corruption," Billy responds.

"You are so right! Your mother and I loved the old system. We worked hard, had a big house, and plenty of money. Now all the government lets us have is a small pay check and the tiny apartment. They will not even allow us to buy a car due to the climate change propaganda, lies, and incorrect weather forecasts. But now we must follow all laws and pretend that we like the new socialist system. Revolution is almost impossible now because the government police force is so huge and they took most of our guns years ago. You know they torture people all the time," Dale said.

President Warner received lavish praise and a new title from the Politburo this week. She was declared "The People's Leader" by the Party leadership to signify her firm grip on power in this one-party nation. Chairman Mao from China would be proud if he were still with us.

"Communism is not love. Communism is a hammer which we use to crush the enemy," Mao Zedong. (4)

Dale and Billy see soldiers and secret service on the roof of the White House and the Blair office building. Machine guns and howitzers are pointed directly at the crowd. Sandbags protect the security personnel. Dale remembers being in the military a long time ago.

They were taught never to point the weapon at civilians. Those times are gone. Nowadays all the guns are pointed directly at the defenseless civilians.

Two blocks from Lafayette Square the riot police are dealing with thousands of protesters. It looks like a scene from Cajamarca, Peru back in 1532. The Spanish rolled in led by Pizarro to expand the kingdom. They slaughtered the Incas led by their Emperor Atahuallpa.

Today the police are beating the young rebels with clubs and fists. Some of the youngsters urinate on themselves in fear and pain just like many did back in 1532. Many are missing hands, legs, and fingers just like the poor Incas. The police sprayed the crowd with automatic machine guns.

Back in 1532, the Incas were unarmed and defenseless against the brutal Spanish with armor, swords, and rifles. Pizarro sent a Friar in to see if the Emperor would subject himself to the law of Jesus Christ and gave him a Bible. The riot police today do not know what a Bible looks like, but are kindred spirits with these evil Spanish soldiers.

The Emperor looked at the Bible and then threw it to the ground. The Friar got really mad. Six thousand Incas died that day. The Spanish imprisoned the Emperor for eight months while extracting a huge ransom for his release. Only 5,400 protesters die today within the District of Columbia. Many more die across the country.

After the Inca filled a 22 by 17 foot room with gold to get their leader back, the Spanish executed poor Emperor Atahuallpa just for kicks. (7)

The victim does not care if the killer has a Bible in his hand or not. Dead is dead and evil is evil.

"Make sure you smile and clap and jump up and down when the Dear Leader rides by in the car in the parade. We must be very enthusiastic in public so the government employees will let us keep our jobs and so you can get into college," Dale said.

"Really? That seems so dumb. I feel like a kid in communist China or North Korea," Billy said.

"Political power grows out of the barrel of a gun," Mao Zedong. (4)

Dale thinks romantically about his SUV that the government took away a while back under the climate change law. It was a 2018 dark blue BMW X5 with fat tires and a turbo engine. Times were good back then in a free-enterprise democracy. He got a deal on the SUV down in Reading for $90,000 and loved it.

"Your mother and I will be fired and put in prison and you will be denied college if The Party folks do not like us or suspect that we want capitalism back. They may even torture us. Please be careful son. Hopefully, this too shall pass. Boy, I miss my BMW," Dale said.

Bibliography

1. Rita Thievon Mullin, "Thomas Jefferson: Architect of Freedom" 2007.

2. David Rubenstein, "The American Story: Conversations with Master Historians" 2019.

3. Burton W. Folsom Jr, "New Deal Or Raw Deal? How FDR's Legacy has Damaged America" 2009.

4. Brainyquotes.com.

5. Wikipedia.org.

6. Frank Dikotter, "How to be a Dictator" 2019.

7. Jared Diamond, "Guns, Germs, and Steel" 2005.

8. The Wall Street Journal.

"What did the Provincial Party Chairman give you when we left the stadium? Was it food?" Tom asks Jane.

"Oh, he gave me a T-bone steak. It is the biggest piece of meat I have ever seen! It is bigger than my mother's cow," Jane replies.

"That is great. Let us eat it right now. My steak was the prettiest piece of meat I have ever seen!" Tom said.

"No, no, I am taking it home to show my parents. They will not believe what the Americans are eating over here. That was delicious. This is unbelievable!" Jane said.

It is January 20, 2025 in Washington, DC, inauguration day in the People's Socialist Republic of the United States (PSROUS). Another rigged election is over. This is a sovereign nation comprised of 27 provinces from the former USA. The government and economy are highly centralized. The southern border runs from southern Virginia to Pennsylvania to Ohio to Indiana to Illinois to Iowa to Nebraska to Colorado to Idaho to Nevada to California.

"We passed the Family Act four years ago which has already raised $900 billion from couples that make more than $70,000 per year. This money has been transferred to millions and millions of low-income